# THE
# BEACHWALKER'S
# GUIDE

# THE
# BEACHWALKER'S
# GUIDE

## The Seashore from
## Maine to Florida

BY EDWARD R. RICCIUTI

*With Drawings
by Suzanne C. Ames*

A DOLPHIN BOOK
Doubleday & Company, Inc., Garden City, New York
1982

BOOK DESIGN BY SYLVIA DEMONTE-BAYARD

Library of Congress Cataloging in Publication Data

Ricciuti, Edward R.
The beachwalker's guide.

"A Dolphin book."
Includes index.
1. Seashore biology—Atlantic coast (United States)
2. Beaches—Atlantic coast (United States)  I. Title.
QH104.R53      574.909'46
3. Tide pool ecology. AACR2
ISBN: 0-385-13051-1
Library of Congress Catalog Card Number 78–68358

# CONTENTS

# THE
# BEACHWALKER'S
# GUIDE

# 1

## *The Atlantic Rim*

The Atlantic margin of the United States is anchored in Maine by bulwarks of rock and slick cobble beaches. Its other end, in Florida, is a thin edge of coral and limestone. Linking these two distinct coasts is a third. It has two faces. Outermost is a broken chain of sandy barrier islands, more than a thousand miles long. Although fragile ecologically, they break the power of the surf. Cradled between them and the mainland is a welter of bays and estuaries, a shielded inner coast of marshes, river mouths, tidal creeks, and lagoons.

As it appears today, the seashore rimming the Atlantic was shaped less than 12,000 years ago, when the last great glaciers of the ice ages melted. Flushed with water, the sea gradually rose and the coast took its present outline, although, to be sure, details have been added since.

Actually, the sea continues to rise, although the advance is imperceptible, barely a fraction of an inch yearly. Many of the changes that go on at the seashore escape notice. The shore has an air of permanence, but that is an illusion. It ceaselessly changes, in ways that are sometimes inconspicuous, other times dramatic.

Storms forge new channels through barrier islands. Sand is carried in by waves, swirled away by wind. Algae stranded on a rock dry and crumble to brown dust. Great cliffs, seemingly impervious, are pulverized by the waves. Bit by tiny bit, they tumble into the water. Beaches build up. Forests claim them and, in turn, vanish under the sea.

Sea and land perpetually contest the shore. The struggle surges back and forth daily, with the tides. On a grand scale, it spans geologic time. Within the past three million years, the location of the Atlantic shoreline has varied at least 100 miles in both directions. A few million years ago, ocean waves rolled over the sites of Washington, D.C., Baltimore, Philadelphia, and New York City. But that was before the Pleistocene ice age. Then, much of the world's water was locked up in glaciers. The sea shrank from the land.

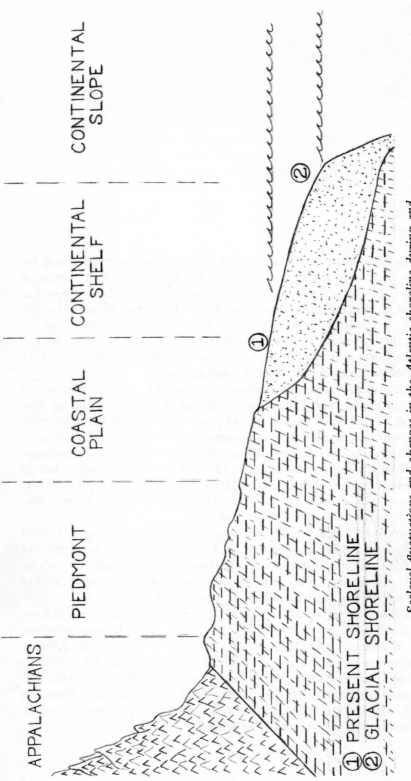

APPALACHIANS | PIEDMONT | COASTAL PLAIN | CONTINENTAL SHELF | CONTINENTAL SLOPE

① PRESENT SHORELINE
② GLACIAL SHORELINE

*Sealevel fluctuations and changes in the Atlantic shoreline during and after the ice ages.*

# THE CONTINENTAL SHELF

About 25,000 years ago, the last and greatest ice age was peaking. What is now the coast was far inland. Beyond was a great sloping plain exposed by the retreating sea. Mammoths, mastodons, and other prehistoric animals roamed the plain, undoubtedly tracked by early hunters. Today, fishermen pursue their catch where the ice-age beasts once roved. The sea has covered the plain again. It is known as the continental shelf. Every coast has one, a lip of land pitched gently from the continental mass toward the ocean abyss.

Technically, the continental shelf is the portion of the sea floor extending from low water to a depth of 100 fathoms. That is equal to 600 feet. In metric terms, the technical boundary of the shelf is rounded off to 200 meters.

Actually, the 100-fathom mark does not always coincide with the real physical boundary of the shelf. This is where the shelf ends at the continental slope. For most of its expanse, the shelf pitches seaward at about 7 to 12 feet a mile. Suddenly, at the edge of the slope, the pitch steepens. It plunges toward the abyss at a rate of up to 500 feet a mile. In many places, this precipice begins at depths much less than 100 fathoms. The shelf is only about 4 miles wide off Florida. Off New York, it extends for more than 100 miles.

# THE SHAPING OF THE SHORE

The rise of the sea that covered the shelf the way it is today began slowly and took a long time. As the sea advanced up the shelf, it left the remains of ancient beaches in its wake. The seashore of today is only the most recent in a series marking the march of the sea inland. Offshore, parallel to the present coast, the remnants of old beaches survive in the form of bands of broken shells. Such "shell hash" is a sign that on a particular spot the surf once pounded to pieces the shells of clams, snails, and similar creatures.

Oceanographers who dredge up shell hash can be sure it was made on a beach if it contains particles called oolites. These form when calcium carbonate from sea water hardens around a grain of sand or speck of shell. It only happens in the shallows.

The rising sea flooded the valleys of rivers that had cut across the shelf. A great valley off Block Island disappeared. Another was filled and became Long Island Sound. The Hudson River valley lost its lower 100 miles. The lower valley of the Susquehanna River was

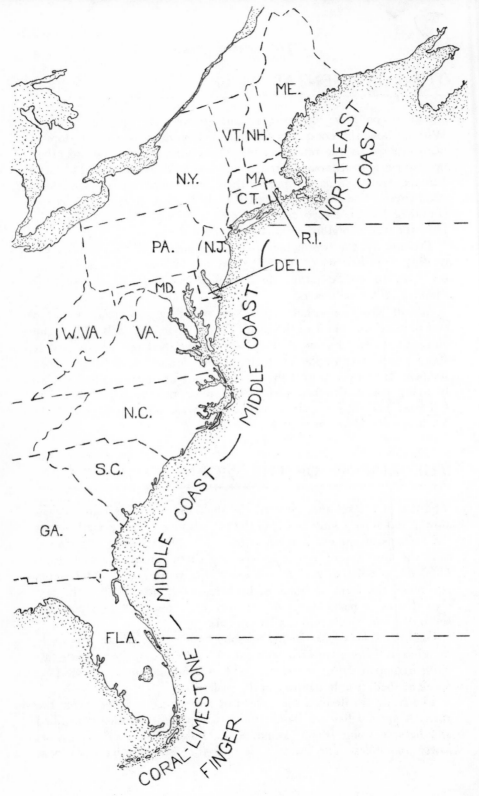

*The Atlantic coast of the United States.*

drowned, too, for 70 miles. The result was our largest estuary, Chesapeake Bay. Shallow and rich in seafood, it covers 3,237 square miles.

## COASTAL ORIGINS

The landscapes that became the three distinct coasts between Maine and the Keys originated quite differently. Of the three, that of New England is especially unique. Its character was sculpted by the ice-age glaciers. They never reached south of the present New York City and Long Island. So none of the vast shoreline south of there—most of the coast, therefore—felt any impact of the glaciers. The landscape remained much as it had before the ice ages. The southernmost seashore of coral and limestone, and the middle coast of sand barriers and estuaries, are ancient. The northern coast—rocky, gravelly, and only touched with sand—is young.

## THE NORTH

Colossal sheets of ice, more than a mile high, slid over the land. The ice bulldozed away forests. It scraped soil from the hard underlying rock, which was left grooved and scratched. With the flowing ice was carried the rubble created by its passage. Boulders, gravel, clay, and sand were transported hundreds of miles. When the glaciers halted and then retreated, they dropped the rubble. It lay in ridgelike heaps, marking the point of the glaciers' farthest advance. At least three times in the last 100,000 years, New England has felt the weight of the glaciers, which left the rubble heaps in their wake.

Especially in New Hampshire and Maine, the coast presents a wall of rock to the waves. Much of the rock along the shore is granite, gray and unyielding. It is the same type that is so evident inland. Granite forms deep in the earth, when molten material called magma solidifies. Sometimes, pressure, heat, and other forces can change the crystalline structure of granite into another form of rock, called gneiss. This rock (pronounced "nice") looks like a streaky sort of granite, and also is common on the northeastern coast.

Granite and gneiss are very hard. Although gouged, they resisted the scraping of the glaciers. They also have withstood the erosion of the surf. The shores of northern New England look much as they did when the glaciers had just surrendered the region.

*This rocky beach in eastern Connecticut typifies the rugged nature of the northeastern coast and at the same time shows how the natural seashore has been changed by development. Rocky seashores in the Northeast are the result of glaciation during the ice ages.*

Strewn about New England shores are boulders that obviously belong to an entirely different type of rock than that around them. In most cases, these boulders were carried to the shore from elsewhere by the glaciers.

Boulders, cliffs, rockpiles, and splintered columns give the northeastern shore a jagged, forbidding visage. Often, the rocks rise sheerly, right out of the water.

Among the rocky coasts, sandy beaches are few and small. Generally they form in sheltered places, such as coves, or the inside of hooks. Often the sand is mixed with rough gravel and large, smooth pebbles called cobble. The pebbly mix comes from glacial debris, material washed inland by the waves, or seaward by rain and streams. Some of the fist-sized rocks also are carried in to shore by seaweeds called kelp. Kelp is a ribbonlike plant with a "holdfast" of fingerlike projections at its base. The fingers anchor the plant to small rocks. Often the plants, with their rocks, wash ashore.

Rocky shores lie south of Maine, too. They are abundant on Cape Ann, Massachusetts, and along the Connecticut coast. But they are not nearly as imposing as in Maine. Most southern New England seashores, particularly from Cape Cod south, are composed of the glacial debris left when the ice retreated. These deposits of rubble formed many of the major land features of the coast. Long Island, Block Island, Fishers Island, Nantucket, Martha's Vineyard, and Cape Cod are built largely of the long, rubbly ridges, which are called moraines.

It is in such areas that you find the only really extensive sandy beaches in the Northeast. If you see this type of beach there, it probably is at the foot of a moraine. Unlike the rockbound coast, the rubbly shore is soft, easily eroded. Waves and wind take the sand for beaches from the moraines. Year after year, the great bluffs crowning

*A closeup of cobble shows how the wave-smoothed stones pack together in a rough, slippery carpet that covers many beaches of the northeastern coast. Cobble is usually close to the water line.*

the beaches of places such as Cape Cod and Martha's Vineyard are being eaten away. The rate is a yard a year in western Martha's Vineyard and southern Block Island.

The glaciers had another profound effect upon the northeastern seashore. They are responsible for the broken, indented shoreline—the myriad coves, headlands, cliffs, and little bays. Again, the handiwork of the glaciers is most graphic in northern New England.

What happened, simply, is that the weight of the glaciers pushed down the land, and tilted it seaward. The rising sea not only flooded the coastal plain but rolled over the sunken terrain into the interior. Water surged up the valleys between mountains whenever the opening presented itself. The shoreline became notched and irregular.

*Spray and surf often freeze into ice along the northeastern coast during the winter. Sea ice—unlike that from fresh water—incorporates salt within the ice crystals. This scene from the shore of Long Island Sound in Connecticut was taken in January.*

# THE MIDDLE COAST

South of the northeastern coast, the seashore is very different. By and large it is flat and smooth, where it directly confronts the ocean. It makes almost no difference whether you face the surf in New Jersey, Maryland, the Carolinas, or almost anywhere else down to southern Florida. Up and down the beach is an unbroken expanse of sand. Behind the sandy strips on the ocean lie all sorts of bays and wetlands. In fact, the Atlantic coast is basically sandy beaches, backed by estuaries, with a northern wing of rock, and a small, coral-limestone finger to the south.

The middle coast begins even amid the glacial remnants. Sandy barrier islands that characterize it begin as far north as Rhode Island and the South Shore of Long Island. In New Jersey, it already is full-fledged.

If you stop a moment on any middle-coast beach and look inland, you will see the geological reason for the character of the middle coast. From the surf to the green foothills of the Appalachians, the terrain is almost all flat and sandy. This is the great Atlantic coastal plain. Now turn and look seaward. Imagine the same type of landscape extending all the way to the edge of the continental slope. This is exactly the case. The coastal plain and the continental shelf are one. At this time, the seaside half happens to be under water. The location of the beach may have varied in the past, but it looked no different.

The barrier islands point southward along the New Jersey coast. Here and there the sea has cut channels through them to the bays behind. Sometimes new cuts are formed, old ones closed, by storms. In 1750, for instance, a raging storm opened a channel through the barrier into Barnegat Bay, largest on the New Jersey coast. By 1812, the sea had closed it again with sand. The bays behind the barrier islands on the southernmost stretch of New Jersey shore have been almost completely filled with salt marshes, a trend that is repeated in areas farther to the south.

Assateague Island, off the eastern shore of Maryland and Virginia, typifies the barrier islands of the middle coast. The story of its origins could be told of myriad similar islands all along the shore. It began when waves sweeping over the gentle plains of the continental shelf dropped sand in the shallows just offshore. A sand bar appeared. It collected more sand from the waves. Onshore winds brought still more sand. At the same time the bar was being shaped by currents running south along the coast. They stretched the bar in a southerly direction. Today the process continues. Sand stolen from the northern end of Assateague Island is building up a hook at the opposite tip.

Assateague became an island as a parade of plants took root. Beach grass began it. Salt-tolerant, this tough grass makes a mat of roots for the windblown seeds of other plants to take hold.

As Assateague grew, the water between it and the mainland took the form of a large bay, edged with marshes. Now, however, the bay is shrinking, because the island is moving toward the mainland. The ocean has eaten 1,000 feet into the beach side of Assateague in the last generation. Meanwhile, the bay side has built up. The process has literally caused the island to move landward across the bay. The ocean beach is now situated where the bay side once was. On the beach can be seen the stumps of a cedar forest that used to grow beside the bay.

Behind the eastern shore that is fronted by Assateague is the country's largest estuary, Chesapeake Bay. It is a trough in the sandy coastal plain. Averaging about 10 miles wide, the bay is 160 miles long. It is fringed in many places with salt marshes, which mark the mouths of rivers and streams.

Below the mouth of the Chesapeake begins the most remote line of barrier islands on the entire coast. These are the Outer Banks. Basically, they are two strips of sand, crescent-shaped, averaging a half mile wide, and extending for a total of 150 miles. The northernmost crescent arches outward and ends where Cape Hatteras juts into the sea. From there the banks curve in concave fashion to Cape Lookout.

While traveling along the banks, you can pass through points which are at least 30 miles from the nearest mainland. Most of the way, you will be hardly above sea level. As a rule the banks are less than 15 feet high. That is, except in a few places where sand dunes rise. Some of them tower to almost 100 feet, the highest on the Atlantic coast.

South of the banks, the barriers edge so close to land that for small stretches they disappear. Then begins a tremendous realm of estuarine salt marshes, interspersed by sounds, that runs all the way from South Carolina to the mouth of the St. Johns River, in Florida. This is truly a marsh world, laced with rivers and creeks. In many places the marshes extend out two dozen miles from the mainland. It is a wilderness of water and soggy tideland, covering 2,000 square miles.

Between the marshes and the sea are more barrier islands. But these are different than the ones to the north. They are not mere strips, but large islands, with considerable field and forest. These are the sea islands, such as St. Catherines, Sapelo, Jekyll, and Cumberland. Some have been turned into resorts. Others have been preserved, virtually pristine, or at least undeveloped. On the ocean side of these large is-

*Wide, sandy beaches characterize the middle coast. In many places on Georgia's sea islands, such as St. Catherines, shown here, the beach is walled by high, sandy bluffs. The shells of clams and oysters eaten by the Indians who once lived on the islands can be found in the sand of the bluffs where waves and wind have eroded them.*

lands lie the same type of long, sandy beaches typical of the more narrow barriers.

The thin barrier islands begin again south of the St. Johns River. They edge most of the Florida shore all the way down to Miami Beach. These barriers were built in much the same way as Assateague Island. Waves brought the sand, and southerly currents shaped it into long bars.

Very long, narrow lagoons, quite shallow, lie behind the barriers. In one of these lagoons, about a third of the way down the Florida shoreline, you can find the first sign that the vast middle coast is nearing its southern end. Growing in Mosquito Lagoon, south of New

Smyrna Beach and north of Cape Canaveral, are the most northerly mangrove trees on the Atlantic coast. Mangroves are scrubby trees, described in detail later in the book, that are able to grow in salt as well as fresh water.

From Mosquito Lagoon south, mangroves grow increasingly thick in bays and estuaries. By the coral-limestone coast of the Keys, mangroves have replaced the salt marshes characteristic of such places to the north.

## THE CORAL-LIMESTONE FINGER

Between the cold times of the Pleistocene, when glaciers held northern North America in thrall, were periods of luxuriant warmth. In one such "interglacial," before the last ice age, southern Florida was covered by up to 120 feet of ocean water. Great reefs of coral grew profusely there, building toward the surface. When the sea level dropped during the ice age, the coral died. The sea has risen again since, but not enough to cover all the remains of that ancient reef, which form the Upper Florida Keys.

Starting at Virginia Key just off Miami Beach, the chain of rocky islets to Big Pine Key are hunks of the old reef that protrude above the surface. Continuing down the chain, to Key West and a handful of tiny islets beyond, the long-dead reef has been covered. Overlying it is a cap of limestone. It formed from sediment—the remains of shells, dead animals, and oolites. Although the reef is the foundation of the Lower Keys, the islands themselves are limestone.

Between the Keys and the mainland lies the shallow expanse of Florida Bay, specked with low islands on which grow thick stands of mangroves. The mainland is flat as a platter. It is fringed with a wilderness of mangroves that on the landward side merges with the freshwater marshes and sloughs of the Everglades.

The Keys are strung out like jewels in a quietly beautiful sea. A rim of offshore reefs shields the Keys from heavy surf. This permits luxuriant mangrove growth, particularly on the even more sheltered bay side. No other part of the Atlantic coast seems so much one with the sea. The Keys have hardly emerged from it. They are surrounded by immense flats, covered by clear water so shallow that you can wade through it for hundreds and hundreds of yards offshore.

# THE EXTRAORDINARY SEASHORE

The Atlantic coast ends in a realm of coral, washed by an easy, warm sea. Its southernmost shores lie literally within a few score miles of the tropics. Its northernmost shores are battered by storms spawned in the Arctic. These extremes, together with the immensity of the sands that span the distance between them, give the Atlantic shores variety that is extraordinary. Few other coasts offer such diversity. Between Maine and the Keys, you can find virtually any type of seashore that exists on earth.

# 2

## A Realm of Zones

Whatever their characteristics, all shorelines share a few key qualities. Two are especially important. Firstly, the shore is what ecologists call an "ecotone." This technical term simply means a place where two drastically different environments meet and interact. Secondly, it is a realm in which life is distributed in zones, from just below the low-water mark to the high ground wet only by the spray.

## A HARSH HOME

The closeness of two environments in an ecotone can provide a wide range of habitats for plants and animals. But it also can make such a place a very harsh home. This is especially true of the shore, a battle-ground of land and sea. Living things find it very difficult to cope with the type of continual and often violent change that characterizes the seashore.

Seashore organisms must be able to handle the smashing power of the surf, the rush and retreat of waves. They must withstand wind-whipped sand. Above all, they must survive the extreme changes in temperature, salinity, and moisture caused by the ebb and flow of the tides.

## WAVES

The endless motion of the ocean is symbolized by waves heaving on the sea. Their impact, even if small, is felt continuously on the shore. To the eyes, a wave may seem to be a crest of water marching toward the land. But this is really not the case. A wave is not water. It is a

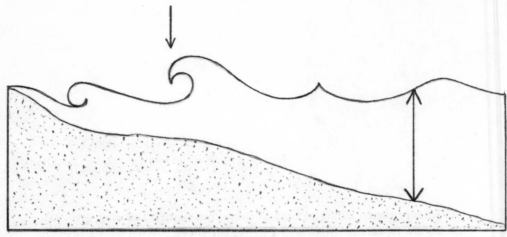

*A breaking wave.*

form of invisible energy, mainly from the wind, moving *through* the water. The crests and troughs visible in the sea reflect the form of the wave as it travels forward. But they stay in place—moving, it is true, but up and down, not ahead.

The water disturbed by a wave moves forward only in the shallows. There, friction slows it on the bottom. The crest, meanwhile, continues to rush ahead, until it breaks. Then the water surges up the beach.

Even a light breeze can spawn waves. One of slightly less than 2.5 miles an hour is enough to produce wavelets. Generally, sea waves are less than a dozen feet high, even on the open ocean. The height, in feet, seldom is more than half the speed of the wind, in miles per hour. Thus, only during great storms such as hurricanes and severe nor'easters, do very high waves slam the shore.

## SEA FOAM

Waves generate tiny bubbles that together, but kept from contact by liquid film, make sea foam. The bubbles in turn are responsible for the salt spray along the shore. As the bubbles surface, they pop. Each time one bursts, a fountain of minute droplets sprays into the air.

# TIDES

Waves keep the shore in turmoil, but its life is governed by the rhythm of the tides, which result from forces generated by the movement of the earth in relation to various celestial bodies. The whole phenomenon is very complex. It is simpler, and sufficient, to say that the main reason for the tides is the gravitational pull of the moon, and less so of the sun.

Because of its nearness, the moon has more than twice the effect on the tides as the sun. The pull of the moon causes two tidal "bulges," one on either side of the earth. As the earth spins, most parts of it pass through both bulges daily. The bulges are the high tides. Between them are the low.

Currents, landforms, the shape of the bottom, and many other local factors influence the tides. For this reason the gap between high and low tide differs from one place to another. In parts of Maine it can be more than a dozen feet. At Cape May, New Jersey, it is four feet, in

*This dab of sea foam was carried more than one hundred yards inland by the wind and dropped in a small cleft among huge boulders on a rocky point in Hammonasset State Park in Connecticut, bordering eastern Long Island Sound.*

portions of Chesapeake Bay less than two feet, and in south Florida two and a half feet.

The most extreme tides occur twice monthly, at full and new moon. This is when the sun and moon are in line and their pulls thus combine. The tides at this time are the "spring" tides, a name that has nothing to do with season. Spring tides are fourteen days apart. After one of them, the tidal range decreases until a low point is reached. This happens seven days after spring tide, at either the first or last quarter of the moon, the time of the "neap" tide. The neap is the middle of the tidal cycle. From then on the tides begin to increase their range until in another week the cycle peaks and the spring tides take place again.

Both daily and two-week tidal cycles orchestrate the distribution of plants and animals at the shore. They tend to be apportioned in a series of horizontal life zones, depending on their ability to survive out of water. The zones differ according to geography and the kind of shoreline on which they are found. All, however, are delineated by the types of organisms which dominate them and all occur within one or another of three basic tidal regions.

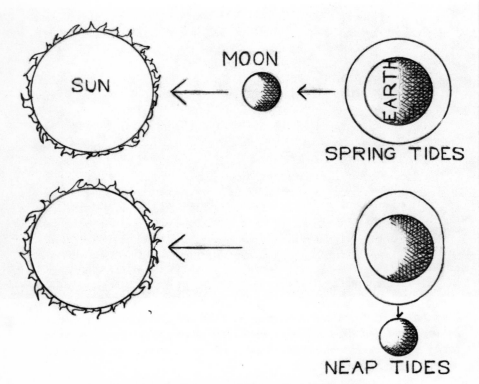

*Astronomical causes of the spring and neap tides.*

# TIDAL REGIONS

Below the low-tide mark is the "sublittoral" region. It is composed of shallows which always are under water, but not deep enough to be immune to the effects of the atmosphere. The temperature of the sublittoral, for instance, fluctuates and compares with that of the air. Between the low-tide mark and high water is the "littoral," or inter-tidal region. This is the area in which plants and animals are confronted with the most dynamic change. Conditions are at best chaotic. The region above the intertidal, from the high-tide line into the dunes, bare rock, or even forest, is the "supralittoral." It is here, just above the high-tide mark, where big heaps of dead plants and animals, seabird feathers, shells, driftwood, and other debris are cast up by the sea. This is the strand line. It is most evident on sandy beaches.

Along rocky shores, on the other hand, the strand line hardly exists. But on the rocks the life zones into which the tidal regions are divided are clearest of all.

# LIFE ZONES—ROCKY SHORES

Life zones are most easily seen on a rock coast for one very good reason. Plants and animals cannot hide below the surface, as on a sandy beach or mud flat. In the Northeast there is an added factor. The great range of the tides creates many belts in which the living conditions are very different from one another. There is room between the low water and the spray for many broad, obviously distinct zones.

A big tidal span, however, is not always necessary for zonation to be displayed graphically. Nor is a great conglomeration of rocks. Consider the middle coast, where tidal ranges are somewhat compressed, and rock areas few, although artificial breakwaters and similar constructions have added to them. The zones can stand out on a single boulder, isolated but subject to the tides. And even if rocks are absent, you can find rocky shore zones on the pilings of bridges or piers.

The nature of a shoreline determines what kinds of organisms live there. Whatever inhabits a rocky coast must be able to anchor on an impenetrable surface and hold on, even in pounding surf. Unable to burrow down when the tide goes out, residents of the rocks must be able to withstand exposure to the air, for long periods if they are in the upper zones.

Of course, the assemblage of plants and animals on shores of rock

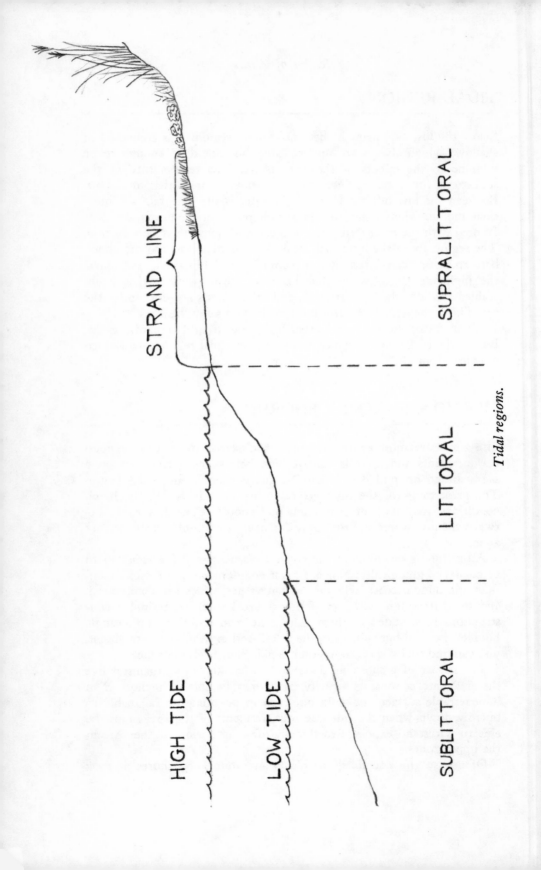

*Tidal regions.*

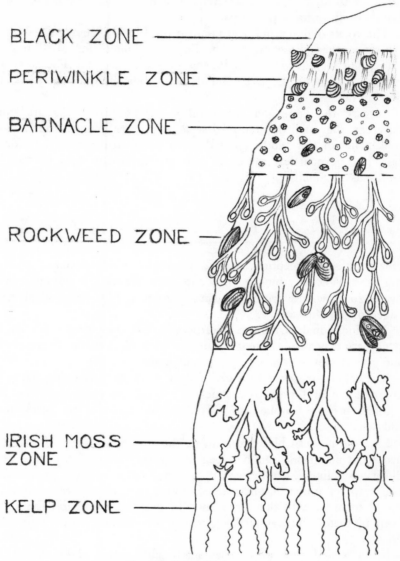

BLACK ZONE

PERIWINKLE ZONE

BARNACLE ZONE

ROCKWEED ZONE

IRISH MOSS
ZONE

KELP ZONE

*Rocky-shore life zones.*

differs according to geography. The range of both species and tides has a lot to do with the character and arrangement of the life zones. Local conditions also play a part.

The rocks of limestone and coral in the Florida Keys, for example, are softer than those up North. They are honeycombed with deep caves, and blanketed with sediment, hiding much life. The tides are gentle, but the sun, with near-tropical radiance, makes the shore fiercely hot.

Because the zones on the coral and limestone rocks are quite different, they will be described separately, later in this chapter. The rock zones of the middle coast differ a bit from those of the Northeast, but nevertheless there are enough similarities for the two to be discussed together.

## THE BLACK ZONE

One zone is an exception because it exists on all rock coasts, even in the Keys. Wet only by the spray and storm waves, it is the uppermost beach zone, where primitive plants known as blue-green algae have edged out of the sea.

The individual plants are microscopic, but they grow in colonies which are easy to see. They resemble a slick black scum on the rocks, and give the level its name, the "black" zone.

It is believed that the blue-green algae were the first living things to colonize the land, perhaps as much as 600 million years ago. The first colonies probably looked no different from those of the black zone today.

Like the modern blue-green algae, the ancient pioneers of the land had to avoid drying out between infrequent moistenings. How they did it, most likely, can be seen upon examination of their present-day counterparts under a microscope. Blue-green algae are coated by gooey material with the consistency of gelatin. It insulates the algae, keeping them moist, as well as making the colonies slippery to walk on.

From New Jersey north, small snails called rough periwinkles (*Littorina saxatilis*) climb up from the zone below to graze in the algae, especially if they are moist. This creature, as long as one's thumbnail, rasps the algae from the rocks with a hard tongue, covered with myriad tiny teeth that make it rough as sandpaper.

The rough periwinkle's wanderings demonstrate that the boundaries of the zones are not totally hard and fast. Many plants and animals can be found outside of the zones of which they are most typical, although not in such abundance as to blur the boundaries of the zones.

## THE PERIWINKLE ZONE

Below the algae, the periwinkles are so thick that the next zone seaward is named for them. The periwinkle zone floods only during the spring tides. The rest of the time, the little snails that throng there must get along with only a light shower of spray. Like other snails, the rough periwinkle can conserve moisture by retreating into its shell and closing the opening with a horny lid. This cover, dark yellow in the rough periwinkle, is called an operculum.

Sealed in the shell, most sea snails can survive out of water for short periods. Sometimes it is only a matter of hours before they perish. The rough periwinkle can last several weeks, and is more like the land snails in this respect. It is similar to the land snails in another way, too. Its young do not hatch from eggs deposited in the water, as is the case with other periwinkles, and indeed, most aquatic snails. Instead, they develop within the parent and emerge fully formed, although so small they hardly can be seen.

The periwinkle zone is the most pronounced on the northeastern coast. As the range of the rough periwinkle approaches its southern end, the zone peters out. It does not exist on most of the middle seaboard.

## THE BARNACLE ZONE

Along middle Atlantic shores, the realm of the acorn barnacles (*Balanus*) lies directly below the black zone. The barnacle zone is under the periwinkle in the Northeast, where it is by far the more impressive.

Masses of barnacles stud the rocks, whitening the surface and making it a forbidding place for those who like to scamper about barefoot. True, not all barnacles inhabit the zone named for them. Some edge even higher on the rocks. Others live near low water, or on ships and whales at sea. But here, in the heart of the intertidal region, the barnacles are supreme.

Twice daily, the strip of shore they inhabit is exposed to the air. For most sea creatures this situation is deadly. But not for the barnacles. They are supremely adapted to it, and thrive.

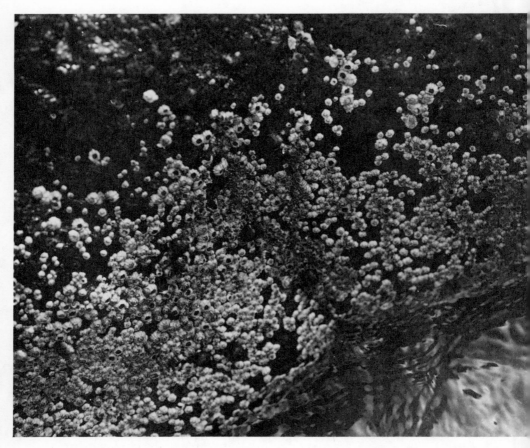

*Mid-tide reveals the barnacle zone of a boulder the size of a kitchen range. Periwinkles rove among the barnacles. The tidal zones on a rocky shore often can be seen on a relatively small boulder.*

When the tide slips away, the barnacle closes the shell that surrounds its small, soft body. Clamped tight within, like a treasure, are stored a few drops of precious moisture, just enough to keep the barnacle from drying out.

Bulwarked against the air, and the cold or heat, the barnacles wait out the low tide. With shells closed, they look as inanimate as the rock beneath them. But in each shell hides a creature resembling a small shrimp. The resemblance is not chance, for like the shrimp, it is a crustacean.

The fortress protecting the barnacle is made of lime, which it has secreted. The construction is ingenious. Six plates, arranged circularly around a flat base, form a cone, open at the top. The gap can be closed by a tight-fitting valve, controlled with muscles stretched between the creature's body and the inner walls of its home.

Within the shell, the barnacle is fixed in a seemingly ludicrous position, for it rests permanently on its head. The absurdity vanishes, however, when the tide comes in and the barnacle feeds. By standing on its head the barnacle can thrust its six feathery limbs out of the shell and sweep the water for food. Microscopic plants and other nourishment are literally kicked into the creature's mouth.

That is about as much as a barnacle moves when adult. It is anchored in place by a glue which fascinates biochemists because it adheres when wet. If it could be synthesized, it would be a boon for surgery and dentistry. Scientists also are interested in what makes the glue work, because they want to find a foolproof way of preventing it from doing so. Removing the barnacles stuck to ships, piers, and other objects now costs millions of dollars annually.

The glue, translucent yellow, is produced by small, goblet-shaped glands. They secrete it just as the barnacle is ready to assume its adult form, attached to a surface. Prior to that, it undergoes several larval stages, different from the adult and free-swimming.

Just before it is transformed into an adult, the barnacle begins to rove over rocks and similar surfaces. It seems to be exploring for the best place to alight. When it finds a spot, it cements itself head down. Within a day, it takes on its adult, shelled form. The shell is so strong it can last long after the barnacle dies, furnishing a shelter for other small sea creatures.

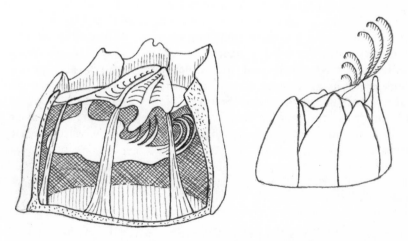

*Acorn barnacle, cross-section and exterior views.*

# THE ROCKWEED ZONE

Below the barnacle belt is a zone characterized by rockweeds, or wrack. There are several kinds. All have air bladders on their branches, or fronds, to buoy them up when they are covered with water. These seaweeds, types of brown algae, usually experience the tidal fluctuations twice daily. During very low tides, however, they can be exposed to air for longer periods.

Two types of rockweed can be especially prominent in the zone. Between New Jersey and North Carolina, only the sea wrack (*Fucus vesiculosus*) grows. Often known as bladder wrack, it sometimes is draped around masses of oysters. From New Jersey north the sea wrack shares the zone with the knotted wrack (*Ascophyllum nodosum*). The two are readily told apart. The knotted wrack has slender branches, often several feet long. Look for it in coves, the insides of breakwaters, and other places sheltered from the heavy surf. The sea wrack, short and broad-branched, can withstand more powerful waves. It is found amid the surf, clinging to rocks, like its relatives, by means of a padlike holdfast.

# THE IRISH MOSS ZONE

Only during the neap tides is this zone uncovered. It is carpeted thickly with purple-red seaweed, Irish moss (*Chondrus crispus*). As its technical name implies, it is rather crispy in texture. About a half foot long, it is formed like a broad, branching tree.

Because it is at the edge of the sea, this zone is inhabited most of the time by true marine creatures, including many small fish. Blue, or edible, mussels (*Mytilus edulis*) attach among the tufted red seaweeds. The mussels have shells that are violet-blue without, and pearly within. They live throughout the intertidal region but congregate in great numbers in the moss zone. South of New Jersey, where the moss does not grow, the mussels remain. Alone, they give the zone their own unique character. They can be found all the way through the Carolinas.

# THE KELP ZONE

The Irish moss zone is the last in the intertidal region. Although it is really part of the sea, the region immediately below the low-water mark is close enough to the shore to be considered a life zone, too. This is especially true from New Jersey north, where the zone is clearly identified by forests of what look like broad brown ribbons, undulating in the waves. These are kelp (*Laminarian agardhii*). The species belongs to a group of brown algae with bladed strands, which in some Pacific kinds grow to more than two hundred feet long.

South of kelp's range, the rocky life zone below low water is rather nondescript and not characterized by any particular dominant organism. The bottom is sand or mud, dotted with sea stars, sea urchins, and various mussels.

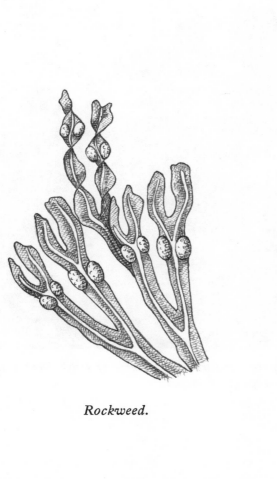

*Rockweed.*

*Kelp.*

*The tidal range along the coral-limestone shores of south Florida and the Keys often is only a matter of inches.*

# CORAL-LIMESTONE ROCK ZONES

The gap between land and sea on the coast's coral-limestone rocks is slight, hardly a foot or two in many places. There is scant room for zonation. The searing sun makes it difficult for any sort of marine life to thrive out of the water. Scattered here and there are various plants and animals, to be described in other chapters, none common enough to create a true zone pattern.

At the lower level of the intertidal region, however, zonation can be seen. In fact, what appears to be rock often is the shells of the creatures that typify the first of these zones.

The shells are the tubular, slightly spiraled constructions of a group of snails. Because of their resemblance to tube-building worms, they are known as "worm shells." They are unlike most other snails because they live in colonies.

Commonest on the coral and limestone rocks are the black worm shells (*Petaloconchus nigricans*). Masses of them gather in the level vacated by the sea only during the lowest tides. Their shells, an inch or so long with the diameter of a drinking straw, are interwoven into a thick tangle blanketing the rock beneath. When the tide is in, the snails within the shells filter minute particles of food from the water.

Lining the low-water mark is another zone of sea urchins (*Echinometra lucunter*) with short spines and the ability to excavate slight holdfasts in the solid rock, or at least so scientists believe. At any rate, anchored in place by their spines they are able to stay put even though lashed by waves. They are so much creatures of the waves that they live only around the surf line.

# TIDE POOLS

On all rocky coasts, from highest to lowest zones, some sea water is trapped in depressions even at low tide. These "tide pools," some mere puddles, are oceans in miniature.

Like the ocean, a tide pool has its own food web. Energy comes from sunlight and is transformed through photosynthesis by green plants—mostly microscopic—into usable food. The plants are consumed by animals of varying size. These in turn are eaten by others. The web spreads, and takes in even gulls and crows, which visit the pools to scavenge, or catch prey such as shellfish.

The pools highest on the shore are least productive. Flooded with fresh water from the rain, they also are highly susceptible to overheating or freezing, as the case may be. Few plants and animals can tolerate such conditions. Tide pools of the littoral region, however, house myriad algae, and animals such as snails, sea stars, sea anemones, sea urchins, sometimes even lobsters and fish.

Tide pools also occur on sandy beaches. There, however, the pools are temporary, because of the fact that a sandy beach is so vulnerable to change.

## THE SANDY BEACH

The face of the sandy beach always is being etched by the wind and water. On smooth sand, each wave leaves a curved line arcing up the beach that marks the extent it surged inland. Just seaward of the limit reached by the waves, tiny holes sometimes appear in the wet sand. These are not made by living things. The holes show where air was released from under the sand as water surged over it. Either waves or wind can make "ripple marks" as they flow over rises in the sand. Once over the top of even a small rise the wave or wind sweeps up more sand and builds a second rise, until several may form in succession.

## MANY SANDS

The sands that compose our beaches are of many varieties. Most contain pulverized shells. The amount varies from only traces on northern beaches to almost 100 percent in the Keys. The shelly materials come from myriad creatures, not only mollusks such as clams and oysters, but even microscopic creatures that drift in the water.

Some sands began as rock deep in the earth, disgorged by geologic upheaval, and crushed. Others are from rock which once belonged to mountains far inland. Pulverized over long ages, it was washed by rains and rivers to the sea. Yet other sands began as glacial debris, dropped by ice sheets on what became the continental shelf.

On the continental shelf, the stuff of which the sands are made is ground up, sorted, sifted, refined, and roiled. Waves sweeping across the shelf bring them to the coast, where they are strewn along the water's edge.

The predominant sand along most of the Atlantic shoreline, above the Keys, is made of quartz. Crystalline, sharp, and light-colored, the quartz makes up more than half of the sand grains on most Atlantic beaches. So hard it lasts almost indefinitely, even in grain form, quartz is, in fact, the world's most common sand. Some beaches on the east coast are almost entirely quartz. White sand, packed hard, is a sign that the mineral is especially abundant.

The quartz sands of northern and middle coast come from the granite of the northern Appalachians. The quartz grains underfoot in Florida originated in the southern part of the mountain chain, and in the Piedmont region of the Carolinas. The distribution of quartz sands in a southerly direction testifies to the trend of currents along the coast.

Other mineral sands sprinkled among the quartz grains dash beaches in many places with color. The hues seen most often are red and black. Black usually comes from magnetite, an iron mix that responds to a magnet. Red, in many shades, generally is garnet, which in large pieces is a semiprecious stone.

Garnet and magnetite are heavier than quartz, which is carried by waves and blown by wind all over the beach. The heavier sands, on the other hand, are dropped well before the high-tide mark. On Assateague Island, for instance, dark smudges of magnetite can be seen about halfway up the beach. The lower and middle reaches of the beaches on Long Island, where garnet is very common, are streaked with red and pink.

## ZONES OF THE SAND

Because a sandy beach is penetrable, and its face continually shifts and moves, the life zones are not as easy to see there as on the rocks. Most of the organisms inhabiting the sandy beach live below the surface, rather than on it. Whereas limpets and chitons clinging to the face of boulders are typical of rocky shores, clams and worms, which burrow deep among the loose grains, characterize the sandy beach. Moreover, it is not possible to find a single organism—such as Irish moss or the periwinkle of the rocks—to delineate a life zone in the sand.

Like the zones of the rocky beach, however, those of the sand are determined by the range of the tides. The zones may span several yards if the tides are great, or just a few feet where there is little distance between the ebb and high tide.

## THE UPPER BEACH ZONE

The portion of the sandy shore that corresponds to the black zone on the rocks is the upper beach zone. It begins at the strand line and,

*Development has taken over the dunes of many beaches along the Florida coast. Where sufficient vegetation remains, however, the dunes may survive.*

depending on the width of the beach, may run a good distance inland or hardly exist at all.

Very often, you can find scattered clumps of a slender grass growing on the upper beach. The vegetation is American beach grass (*Ammophila brevilgulata*), which, as will be explained in a later chapter, forms thick meadows a short distance farther back from the beach front.

The grass is a key part of the matrix that holds the sandy beach together. The clumps, composed of up to a dozen grass stalks each, are linked by a network of underground stems called rhizomes, and anchored by long roots. Rhizomes can extend for as much as fifteen feet out from a plant. The rhizomes and roots together form a mat under the grass which can reach down for six feet, and serves as a trap that catches the sand and prevents it from being stolen by erosion.

*American beach grass waves in the wind on a Connecticut shore. The grass is the "cement" that holds the sand of the dunes in place. No plant of the sandy beach is more important to its stabilization. The death of just a few clumps of beach grass eventually can lead to the destruction of the beach by wind and wave.*

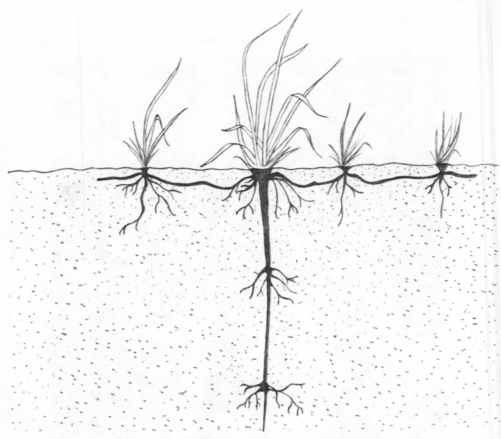

*American beach grass with roots and rhizomes.*

The roots and rhizomes are very sensitive to compaction. If damaged in this way they can die. Another way in which beach grass is vulnerable is that it snaps easily. The stems have a hard covering that permits the plant to resist salt and desiccation, twin threats to plant life so near the sea. The covering, however, makes the stems brittle. They readily snap off at the base, killing the plant. For these reasons, foot traffic—and even worse, vehicles—is very dangerous to beach grass.

When the grass dies, the beach is at the mercy of the wind. It begins to blow away the sand, starting a cycle of destruction. The roots of the grass are exposed, causing more of it to die. In turn the wind takes away more sand. If a storm occurs, waves can breach the gap in the beach created by the wind. The beach will be undermined. Eventually, an entire beach can be threatened because of the initial loss of a clump or two of beach grass. Beaches are but temporary creations. They can be destroyed, just as they are built, by the whim of wind and wave. When humans damage the beach environment, they tip the balance in favor of destruction.

## THE MIDDLE BEACH ZONE

The main zone of the sandy shore is the "middle beach." It takes up virtually all of the littoral region. Seemingly barren, the sands of the middle beach hide a great variety of animals. The types surviving there either burrow into the sand to avoid exposure at ebb tide, or move down the beach with the tide.

## THE SUBTIDAL ZONE

The subtidal region also is synonymous with a life zone on the sandy beach. It is the zone of the shallows, where creatures such as clams burrow beneath the water-covered sand and mud. At any stage of the tide, fish can be found here, signifying the beginning of the true marine environment.

## SALT-MARSH LIFE ZONES

The salt marshes that lie behind the sandy barriers and in estuaries are prominently zoned. Each marsh has three life zones, which lie between the lower portion of the intertidal, and upper boundary of the supratidal regions. Closest to the sea is the zone of mud flats, exposed only at lowest tide. Next is the low-marsh zone, covered by the average high tide, and under considerable water during the spring tides. Even then, however, the tips of a tough, long-leaved grass rise above the water. This is salt-marsh cordgrass (*Spartina alterniflora*), which clearly marks the zone.

Cordgrass serves the marsh much as beach grass helps the dunes. The roots and rhizomes of the cordgrass form a matrix holding the marsh mud in place. Sometimes taller than a big man, cordgrass is vivid green, and reaches peak growth by late summer. During the winter, its leaves decay and are washed away. The stumps of the stems, a few inches high, are all that remain to dot the marsh mud.

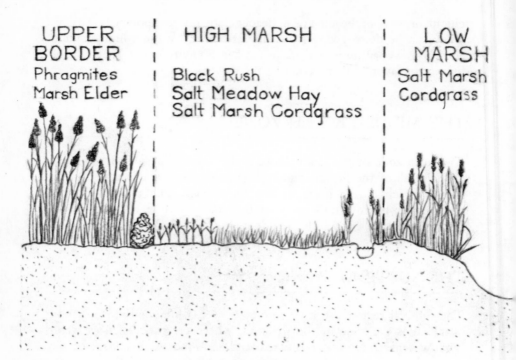

| UPPER BORDER | HIGH MARSH | LOW MARSH |
|---|---|---|
| Phragmites | Black Rush | Salt Marsh |
| Marsh Elder | Salt Meadow Hay | Cordgrass |
| | Salt Marsh Cordgrass | |

*Salt-marsh life zones.*

When spring comes, however, the new shoots arise, fresh and green. By August, the cordgrass has bloomed, with small white flowers.

Cordgrass is an unusual plant because it can live even though flooded twice daily by salt water. It survives because it can extract fresh water from that which surrounds it. Glands in the plant remove the salt from water which has entered through the roots. The salt is excreted through the leaves, which often are speckled with it.

Just beyond the reach of all but the storm tides grows another grass. It signifies the beginning of the high-marsh zone, really the edge of the uplands. The grass is salt-meadow hay (*Spartina patens*), which farmers in some places still mow. Almost a yard high, the hay is light green in summer. Because its stems are weak, it tends to bow as it grows. By August, purple flowers appear on it, and as winter approaches, it browns. All winter it stands, drab and sere. In the spring, the dead grasses fall to the mud. They make a mat which protects the young green shoots of the next crop.

*Salt-marsh cordgrass.*

*New England salt marshes such as this one are generally not as extensive as those farther south, along the middle coast, especially behind barrier islands. Tidal creeks lace such marshes, which are extremely productive areas in terms of plant and animal life.*

Whether a marsh is mostly cordgrass or salt-meadow hay depends on how much of it is in the intertidal region. This, of course, depends on the height of the adjacent land, and the tidal range.

The cordgrass is the key to the tremendous productivity that is characteristic of the salt marsh. Many animals, including insects and crabs, feed directly on the grass. More important, the dead grass is broken down by bacteria into a mixture of fine particles called detritus, which feeds a vast assortment of animals, from microscopic types to oysters and fish. Detritus also nourishes the minuscule plants which are the first link in the entire marine food chain. Thus the influence of the salt marsh is felt far from its borders.

*Cordgrass is beginning to grab a foothold along this sheltered shore on the coast of Connecticut. If undisturbed, small patches of grass such as this can eventually build into a salt marsh. The grass needs some protection—such as a barrier island or bay—from the pounding surf.*

## MANGROVE ZONES

A tremendous amount of detritus also pours out of the seaside forests of mangroves that replace the salt marshes in southern Florida. The mangrove forest parallels the salt marsh in several ways. Like the marsh, the forest is astir with life. From their roots to their crowns, the mangroves harbor a profusion of sea and land animals. The forest also has zones which are clearly marked, in this case by the mangroves themselves.

Closest to the sea are the red mangroves (*Rhizophora mangle*). They stand twenty feet high in the lower intertidal region. Identification of this species is easy. It has glossy-green elliptical leaves. More dramatic, it has large prop roots that arch out from the branches, often from many feet above the ground. The roots hold fast on sand

*The arching prop roots of red mangroves can be easily seen in this thicket along a tidal creek in the Florida Keys. Much of the southern tip of Florida around Florida Bay consists of mangrove swamps. They are the counterpart of northern salt marshes.*

bars, reefs, and oyster beds. They trap mud and silt, as beach grass holds the sand, and promote the development of islands.

Behind the "red mangrove" zone are two others, distinguished by trees that also are called mangroves, but really are unrelated to the red type. Black mangrove (*Avicennia nitida*) grows in the zone behind the red, on ground flooded only during the higher tides. The black mangrove, really a member of the verbena family, is identifiable by an adaptation to seaside living called the pneumatophore. This is a pencil-like projection of the root which sticks up out of the mud, helping the plant respire. A legion of pneumatophores grows around every black mangrove, like thin fingers poking out of the ooze.

The black mangrove grows about the same height as the red. Its leaves also are elliptical. Like the cordgrass, the black mangrove secretes salt through its leaves, which often are dotted with the white compound.

Inshore of the "black mangrove" zone is that of the white mangrove. It grows from the high-tide mark inland, where it often mixes with other vegetation. Shrubby, and in a family with buttonbush, white mangrove marks the innermost boundary of the seashore.

# 3

# The Water's Edge

Especially at low tide, secrets await discovery everywhere at the water's edge. Countless natural vignettes can be observed in the roiled sand, among the rocks, or on the slick mud. Beyond the shallows, of course, is the sea, dominating the scene.

## SEA SALTS

As everyone knows, the sea is salty. But it is less well known that some parts of the sea are much more salty than others. As a rule, the open ocean has a salinity of about 35 parts per 1,000. However, the salinity of inshore waters can be much less. That of the Baltic Sea, almost landlocked and flushed by rivers, is not more than 7 parts per 1,000. The Red Sea, on the other hand, has a salinity above 42 parts per 1,000. There even is a famed "hole" in the Red Sea, more than 6,000 feet deep, where the water is nearly saturated with salt. Its salinity is 270 parts per 1,000.

There are dozens of elements and five main salts dissolved in sea water. Seventy-eight percent of the salt is sodium chloride, the common table variety. Originally, the sea drew its salts from the primeval rock beneath it. Since the ocean was formed, however, more salts have been drained off the land, and the sea has gotten slightly more saline.

## THE COLORS OF THE SEA

Like Joseph's coat, the sea has many colors. The open ocean, however, is blue, and for the same reason the sky is. Tiny particles in both air and water deflect, or scatter, the light waves in sunlight. Shorter wavelengths are scattered more. Since blue happens to have the shortest wavelength of visible light, it is the dominant color in the water. This is especially true where the water is deep enough to restrict reflection from the bottom. In the shallows, sunlight reflected off the bottom can make the water greenish, or even yellow. Inshore waters also may be brown with silt washed from the land. Other hues, such as milky or red, can be caused by throngs of microscopic plants.

## RED TIDE

Mass blooms of microplants called dinoflagellates, for instance, create the infamous red tide. Red tide is the name for sudden outbreaks of discolored water that have killed countless fish and other sea creatures between New England and Florida. The dinoflagellates are believed to produce poisons, and also clog the gills of fish. When the tiny plants die, moreover, they cause fatal deoxygenation of the water.

Dinoflagellates get their name from the two flagella, or whiplike appendages they carry. Like other plants, they carry on photosynthesis. But, astoundingly, they also swim, and some even prey on other tiny organisms in the sea. They multiply out of control in warm water filled with nutrients. The red tide is caused by only a few types, notably a mite that is technically known as *Gymnodinium brevis*.

## PHOSPHORESCENCE

Other dinoflagellates cause the "phosphorescence" that sometimes makes the water sparkle at night, especially when there is no moon. The living light of these dinoflagellates resembles that of fireflies. It is caused by a mysterious chemical reaction, which seems to occur in the dinoflagellates when the water around them is disturbed.

Because dinoflagellates are most abundant in warm waters, "phosphorescence" is usually seen only in the summer along northern coasts. In southern Florida, however, it is common the year around. Some tropical bays have such large dinoflagellate populations they seem to burn with ghostly flame after dark. Two notable ones are in Puerto Rico. Sometimes the light is so bright it is enough to illuminate newsprint in the dark.

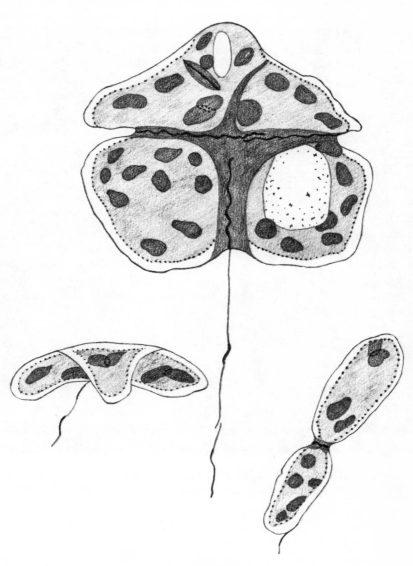

*Gymnodinium brevis.*

*Turtlegrass beds grow in the shallow, sandy flats off the Florida Keys. The grass beds teem with life, ranging from tiny shrimp to giant sea turtles.*

# GRASSES OF THE SEA

Although almost all the plants in the sea are simple, like dinoflagellates and algae, a few advanced forms from the land have strayed beyond the shore and become truly marine. Among these are a hodgepodge group commonly known as "sea grasses."

The most abundant member of this group along the northeastern and middle coasts, to North Carolina, is eelgrass (*Zostera marina*). Despite its name, it is not a true grass, although to the casual glance it resembles one. Really related to pondweeds, eelgrass has long, narrow leaves, sometimes two yards long, which look like green ribbons. Like the other sea grasses, eelgrass grows on flats in the shallows. Sometimes it is so thick it impedes wading.

Along the coasts of Florida, especially in the south, the shallows and reef flats are covered with beds of other sea grasses, all, like eelgrass, true flowering plants. Within the intertidal region is shoalgrass (*Diplanthera wrightii*), which is short and stubbly. From the low-water mark out to beyond wading depth grows turtle grass (*Thalassia testudinum*), recognized by its broad blades. It is the major grass of the coral-limestone coast.

The sea-grass beds provide shelter and food for a multitude of marine animals. There are no better places on the seashore to find sea creatures, including many fish.

# FISH BY THE SHORE

Most shallows within a few feet of the water's edge, in fact, host a surprisingly large variety of fish. Many of them are the young of food and game species. The fingerlings of the spotted sea trout (*Cynoscion nebulosus*), for example, spend their first summer on the grassy flats of the southern coast. The young blackback flounder (*Pseudopleuronectes americanus*), can be found in puddles left on sandy beaches during ebb tide. At high tide, the adult blackbacks, also called "winter flounder," sometimes come into only a few feet of water hunting for food. They usually lurk on mud or sand bottoms, often near eelgrass. In the winter they lie in the mud of bays and river mouths.

## FLOUNDERS

Flounders are noted for having both eyes on the same side of the head. But they do not begin life this way. All of the many kinds of flounders start out with an eye on each side of the head, like other fish. As a flounder grows, however, one eye actually migrates over to rest beside the other. Whether the right or left eye moves depends on the species. The eye that travels in the blackback flounder is the left, so both eyes are on the right side.

The blackback flounder rests on the bottom with its eyed side up. That side is dark brown, with a reddish tinge, and lightly spotted. The hue darkens or lightens to match the bottom on which the fish hides. The eyeless side is snow white.

## TOMCOD

North of Virginia, especially along rocky shores, lives a miniature cod, seldom weighing more than a pound. This is the tomcod (*Microgadus tomcod*), which often can be spotted in just a few inches of water, at the shore's edge. The time to look for the tomcod is in the winter, when it comes in to spawn around the mouths of rivers. Then, usually at night, it can be seen in the water quite easily in the beam of a flashlight. It looks just like a tiny cod, except for a more rounded tail. The ventral fins, below the "chin," end in threadlike projections. The color is grayish-brown above, and yellowish-gray below. The tomcod also is called the "frostfish," because of its abundance in winter, when most other fish disappear.

## AMERICAN EELS

Hugging the shore, and coming into the intertidal with high water, are some of the world's most noted voyagers, the American eels. The eels that are found in our waters begin life in the Sargasso Sea, deep within the legendary Bermuda Triangle. After hatching, the young eels head for the continental coast. The journey takes about a year, during which the growing eels change shape several times. They have become pencil-like elvers by the time they reach the coastal waters.

The eels inhabit almost every kind of shore, but are especially numerous among seaweeds and grasses. Most of the eels that stay

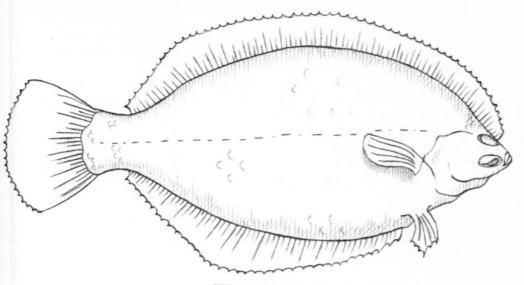

*Winter flounder.*

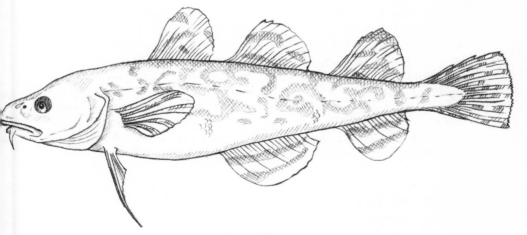

*Tomcod.*

along the coast are males. Females generally travel up rivers, some-times hundreds of miles inland. They even can wriggle overland for short distances.

For up to twenty years, the females stay in freshwater lakes, ponds, and streams. Then they head back out to sea, with the males, to spawn in the Sargasso, and die.

Although eels sometimes reach five feet long and over a dozen pounds, most are smaller. Generally they are only a few feet in length and weigh about a pound or two. They are most active in warm weather. When it is cold they retreat into the mud at the bottom.

## SEA HORSES AND PIPEFISH

Amid the grasses and seaweed live sea horses and pipefish. Members of the same family, Syngnathidae, they share a long, tubular snout, and an exceedingly strange way of reproducing. The males are the sex that becomes pregnant.

On the underside of the male's body is a pouch in which the female places her unfertilized eggs. After fertilization, the embryos develop in the pouch until they are perfect miniatures of the adults. Then they pop from the pouch, one at a time, into the water. Sometimes as many as 150 young may be "born" this way.

The shape of a sea horse is well known. The pipefish is not so famil-iar. It resembles a sea horse that has been stretched to the extreme. At close glance, it can be seen that the body of the pipefish is hexagonal in front, and has four sides to the rear. If you pick up a pipefish, it will wrap its slender but hard body around your hand. This is how it holds on among the underwater vegetation. The sea horse anchors it-self by its prehensile tail, which can curl around a holdfast and grip it tightly.

Sea horses and pipefish hide in the vegetation to ambush small crus-taceans and other tiny prey. These are sucked into the tiny mouth at the end of the long snout that typifies both fish. They are found all along the coast, but are most abundant and varied in the South.

## SMALL BOTTOM FISH—SOUTH

Several other oddly shaped fish, mostly of finger length, inhabit the shallows at the water's edge. As a rule they are long of body, often with big heads and bulbous eyes. They dwell on or close to the bot-

*Sea horse.*

tom, right up into the intertidal during high water.

Along rocky and coral shores in the South are found the Molly Miller (*Blennius cristatus*), and the related seaweed blenny (*B. marmoreus*). Both eat algae and have dorsal fins running almost the full length of the body.

The body of the Molly Miller is dark green, with a strong barred pattern. It seldom strays north of Florida. The seaweed blenny is yellowish on the back and blue-gray below. It sometimes ranges as far north as the Middle Atlantic states, but like the Molly Miller is most common in the South. Look for it among holes and cracks.

On rocky or muddy bottoms from the Carolinas south lives the frillfin goby (*Bathygobius soporator*). It is characterized by a double dorsal fin. Dark-colored, it commonly is stranded in tide pools. Like many other fish that spend part of their lives virtually aground, the frillfin goby can travel overland. It is known for its ability to jump, several feet in some cases.

## SMALL BOTTOM FISH—NORTH

The snakelike body that is an adaptation to creeping among the rocks and on the bottom is a trait of many small, shallow-water fish in the North, too. The rock eel (*Pholius gunnellus*) can be seen along the low-water mark, especially among the kelp and under stones. It is yellowish brown, and resembles a small eel, although it is an entirely different type of fish. The rock eel's dorsal fin is especially long, and edges its back from head to tail. The rear half of the fish's underside also is edged with fin.

The radiated shanny (*Ulvaria subbifurcata*) is a brown fish similar in appearance and dwelling places to the rock eel, although it also roves deeper waters offshore. The shanny can be distinguished by a dark blotch that stands out against the light color of its dorsal fin.

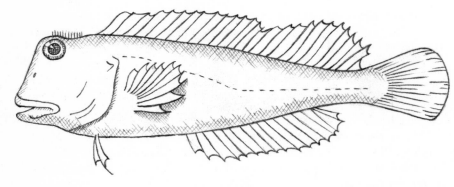

*Molly Miller.*

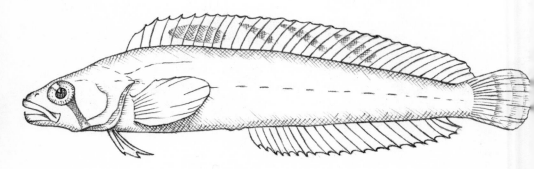

*Radiated shanny.*

# SCHOOLING FISH

Unlike bottom fish, which generally are slow swimmers, fish that school are usually built for speed. Theirs is the torpedolike, or "fusiform" shape, which slips through the water with little resistance. It evolved in fish about 300 million years ago.

Up and down the coast, schools of small fish called silversides (Atherinidae) flash in the shallows, up into the intertidal. They can be glimpsed close to the surface over grass beds, along breakwaters, and in creeks, but not where the surf pounds on open rocks. As their name implies, their blue-green bodies, up to about five inches long, have gleaming sides. Most of the time they live within a few feet of the shore, in less than six feet of water, although cold weather may drive them deeper.

The Atlantic silversides, also called whitebait or shiner (*Menidia menidia*) ranges from Maine to Cape May. The waxen silversides (*M. breyllina*) lives as far south as the Carolinas. In Florida can be found the reef silversides (*Allanetta harringtonesis*) and the hardhead silversides (*Atherinomorus stipes*).

Other little fish that follows the tide are mummichogs, or killifish. They live all along the coast, and commonly are called "minnows." The body of the mummichog is fusiform, but stouter and more rounded than that of the silversides.

The common mummichog (*Fundulus heteroclitus*) is more apt to be seen in salt marshes and so will be described in a later chapter. Along sandy beaches, from Massachusetts south, however, the striped mummichog (*F. majalis*) can be found. It is more slender than the

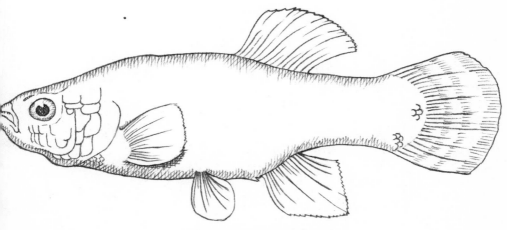

*Common mummichog.*

*A school of fish executes a right turn.*

common "mummy," and is olive green with stripes. The stripes are vertical on males, while females are striped horizontally.

Sometimes striped mummichogs can be found in sandy tide pools, where they have been stranded. They may wait for the tide to advance again and free them. Or, if the pool heats up, they may burrow into the mud. Occasionally, they even spring and wriggle back to the sea.

## WHY FISH SCHOOL

Mummichogs and silversides are but a few of the fish that school. This behavior exists in about four thousand species, large as well as small. It seems to promote survival. A school of small fish, for example, may look to an enemy like a single large animal. Fish in a school tend to move as one, parallel to one another, and in the same direction. The outline of the school tends to remain in the same geometrical pattern.

Generally all the fish in a school are of similar size and thus age. They probably keep together by sensing one another's vibrations as they move through the water. Vision may help too. Many schooling fish have shiny sides, which seems to be a visual aid to staying together.

A school has no leaders, and can turn quickly by a simple flanking movement. Thus, if one member of a school detects a meal and turns toward it, the entire group also may turn and benefit from the food.

## LARGE FISH AT WATER'S EDGE

Occasionally, even very large fish can be sighted within a few feet of the beach. The voracious bluefish (*Pomatomus salatrix*) sometimes even pursues smaller fish right up into the wave wash. It ranges from Maine to Florida, moving north with the summer. Some bluefish exceed twenty-five pounds, but most are smaller. Late in the summer, harbors are filled with the smelt-sized young, or snapper blues, which make exceptionally good eating.

Bluefish in turn are hunted by the sand tiger shark (*Carcharias taurus*). Rarely venturing to the tide line, this shark lives all year around in southern waters and ranges as far north as New England in the summer. It sometimes is referred to, rather contemptuously, as the "sand shark," and considered an innocuous pest. Admittedly, it is not known to bother people, but it reaches eight feet in length, and some of its relatives are known maneaters. Like other large sharks, it should be left alone.

Truly harmless is the smooth dogfish (*Mustelus canis*), a shark that reaches about a yard to five feet in length, and also occasionally comes close to the beach. It also is found dead on sand beaches, sometimes rather frequently.

Also known as the "sand shark," this dogfish has twin dorsal fins, without spines, unlike its relative the spiny dogfish (*Squalus acanthias*), and a round, snubbed snout. It has tiny flat teeth for crushing the shells of lobsters, and ranges from Cape Cod south.

Once in a while, rays also come close to shore. Courting rays sometimes chase one another right into the surf. Two such rays caused a brief scare on a South Carolina beach. Nose-to-tail, they raced through the foam, in a foot or so of water. They moved so much in concert they appeared to be one large fish, like a shark. Bathers raced for the shore.

Even the huge but inoffensive Atlantic manta ray (*Manta birostris*), twenty-two feet across its "wings," sometimes wanders into wadable waters. In Fort Lauderdale, Florida, for example, a big manta swam for the better part of an hour within a few yards of the shore. It seemed confused, and circled continuously. Finally a bather—who apparently realized the awesome fish was no danger—waded out and guided it back out to sea.

## MOLE CRABS

Along the sandy beaches of the middle and southern coasts, the edges of the waves seem aboil with tiny, scurrying creatures, which seem to appear and then disappear in the sand. These are "sandbugs," or more properly mole crabs, among the many crustaceans of the water's edge.

The mole crab (*Emerita talpoida*) is a pill-shaped animal the color of the sand, about an inch long. Great bands of mole crabs follow the water's edge with the tide, for this is where they feed. Facing the waves, they burrow backward into the sand, until only their heads and featherlike antennae extend. As the last of the wave washes back down the beach, the crabs strain minute organisms from the water, then eat them.

The time to look for mole crabs is after the wave has peaked on the beach, and has almost slipped back to the sea. This is when they pop

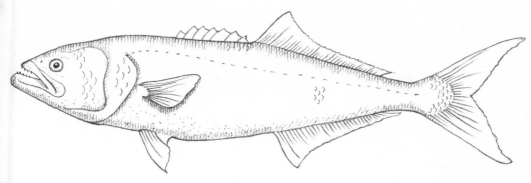

*Bluefish.*

*Often called the "sand shark," and confused with the smaller, inoffensive dogfish, the sand tiger shark sometimes wanders into the shallows as far north as New England. While not generally considered dangerous to humans, it definitely should be left alone because it is of the size and disposition to be hazardous.* (Photo: New York Aquarium)

from the sand. The little creatures are always on the move, keeping abreast of wave and tide.

Sometimes mole crabs are stranded behind the falling tide. Then they burrow into the wet sand and stay there until the water rises again. If you happen to find a mole crab in the sand and notice that its body is soft, rather than hard-shelled, it probably has just molted, or shed its covering. A new one will harden over its body.

The lower beach is often littered with the cast-off shells of mole crabs, as well as their remains. The small crustaceans are a favorite food of many shore birds.

A mole crab with an orange mass on its abdomen is a female with eggs. The eggs hatch while she carries them, and the young crabs, looking nothing like the adults, drift out to sea.

## HERMIT CRABS

Every kind of shore, all along the coast, is populated by hermit crabs (Paguridae). Soft-bodied, the hermit crab anchors its rear into the empty shells of snails and similar mollusks, with its head, pincers, and legs for walking protruding from its home. If need be, the hermit can retreat almost completely into the shell, blocking the entrance with its large pincers. As the hermit crab grows larger, it looks for a shell that is more roomy. Sometimes the crabs will fight over the rights to a shell.

The shells inhabited by hermits range from the size of a pea to a fist. The smaller crabs usually are found closer to shore. Look at low tide, in pools, among the crevices of boulders, and on sand flats.

## TRUE CRABS

The creatures that most come to mind when the word "crab" is mentioned belong to this group, characterized by bodies that are roughly triangular in shape, and large, sharp pincers. The true crabs include those that are most in demand for the table.

Spring and summer on the northern and middle coasts bring the rock crab (*Cancer irroratus*) up to the shore from deep water. Despite its name, it is found on sandy and gravelly shores as well as on the rocks, where it haunts the Irish moss and kelp zones. It has a shell that is yellow, marked with red dots.

Similar to the rock crab, but much more ruddy and robust, is the

Jonah crab (*C. borealis*). Powerful and tough, this crab inhabits the northern portion of our coast. It scuttles about the rocks, even those battered by the full force of the surf.

Inhabiting muddy bottoms, among shellfish beds, near docks, and on pilings are dull-colored creatures known as mud crabs (Pilmunidae). Especially common along the middle and southern parts of the coast, these crabs are slow-moving creepers and crawlers.

Other crabs that seem to move in slow motion are the spider crab (*Libinia emarginata*) and its relative, the toad crab (*Hyas coarctatus*). The toad crab lives north of Cape Cod, the spider crab south of there. Both crabs really do look like spiders, with very long, spindly legs and pincers that are small compared to those of the other true crabs. The legs of large spider crabs may span a foot or more.

Spider crabs have a curious habit of decking themselves out with bits and flags of seaweed, and for this reason sometimes are called decorator crabs. They pick the weed, and glue it to their knobby backs with a secretion made in the mouth. Sometimes tubeworms and other sea creatures, as well as algae, actually grow on the shells of the crabs. It all makes for excellent camouflage.

The lower zones, and the deeper water beyond, are the home of spider and toad crabs. They lurk in grass beds, and amid the kelp.

None of the crabs mentioned above rate as good swimmers. One family of true crabs, however, truly excels at swimming. In fact, its members are known as the swimming crabs.

Most familiar of the swimmers is the blue crab (*Callinectes sapidus*) which ranges from New England south and is the pride of the Chesapeake Bay. (When it molts its shell and has not had time to form a new one, it is called the "softshell.") Delectable to eat, the blue crab is a blue-green creature that can be seen in the shallows, especially around eelgrass, and in the mouths of streams and rivers. Bottoms covered with mud, sand-and-gravel, and sand-and-shells are also good places to look for blue crabs, which are agile, fierce predators.

Among the favorite prey of blue crabs are the smaller fiddler crabs (*Uca*), which wander over mud flats. To watch blue crabs hunt fiddlers is to witness scenes of unbridled ferocity. The blues lurk in the water at the very edge of the flats, motionless but ready to pounce upon the first fiddler that strays within a foot or so of their ambush. When a fiddler does happen by, the blue crab that is nearest explodes from the water, rushes across the mud, and seizes the hapless fiddler in its pincers. In a flash it tears the fiddler to pieces and crams it into its mouth.

Blue crabs thrive in water that is not quite as saline as the open ocean. For this reason they congregate in bays and estuaries. Their marvelous swimming ability is made possible by the shape of the last pair of legs, which resemble paddles.

The lady crab (*Ovalipes ocellatus*) also has a pair of paddlelike legs for swimming. Ranging from Cape Cod south, this crab inhabits sandy beaches, just below the waters edge, where it often buries itself to wait for the small fish it likes to eat. The crab is beautifully colored. Its shell is light purple, often with a yellow tinge, and spotted with dark red.

The swimming legs of the green crab (*Carcinus maenas*) are flat, but not as paddle-shaped as those of other swimming crabs. Never-

*The spider crab is a long-legged creature that festoons itself with bits of seaweed. It is related to the giant king crab of the northern Pacific. The meat of the spider crab is as tasty as that of the king crab but because of the former's small size it is not a popular food item.*

*The blue crab, found from New England south, is especially abundant in the rich, shallow waters of Chesapeake Bay. When the blue crab molts—that is, sheds its shell to grow a larger one to accommodate for growth—it is known and marketed as the "soft-shell."*

theless, the green crab swims proficiently. It is found on the lower portions of rocks, in tide pools, and just below low water, among the eelgrass beds and kelp.

Hordes of green crabs sometimes rove mussel beds, tearing at the flesh of shellfish they find open. The frenzy of feeding brings mummichogs and silversides, which try to share in the banquet, but often are caught by the crabs and themselves eaten. It is not uncommon to see a swarm of crabs, some with chunks of fish in one pincer, fighting over the mussels, while masses of fish school around them.

These crabs are colored muddy green, and usually are only a few inches across. Be careful. They will attack your finger immediately with their sharp pincers if given the chance. Fishermen who use green crabs for tautog bait generally break off their claws before hooking them.

*A green crab stares balefully from a small tidepool on the New England coast. This creature is an active predator that can catch small fish. When threatened, it defends itself with its claws, which can deliver a nasty pinch to a human toe or finger.*

# THE HORSESHOE CRAB

On sand beaches all along the coast, this big creature comes ashore in spring and summer to breed. The female horseshoe crab (*Limulus polyphemus*), often almost two feet long, often is followed by one or more males. Sometimes a male—the smaller sex—may cling to her from behind as she crawls up the beach to the high tide mark to dig a hole for her eggs, often as many as a thousand of them.

After the male fertilizes the eggs, and the incoming tide adds more sand over them, they develop for several weeks before hatching. The hatchlings are tiny but resemble the adults, except for the lack of the spikelike tail. Shortly after escaping from the egg, the young head for the water.

About the only time you will find live horseshoe crabs on the beach outside the mating season is when they are stranded. If beached on its back, a horseshoe crab is in mortal danger. Gulls will spot it and feed on its gills. These structures are easy to see. Look behind the legs, to the rear, for a half-dozen pair of plates that overlap, like the pages of a book.

When a crab is bottom side up, its stiff tail becomes handy. Set in a socket, the tail is movable, and the crab uses it to lever itself over onto its legs. Then it crawls back to the water.

Commonly known as a "living fossil," the horseshoe crab has not changed since at least the time of the earliest dinosaurs, 200 million years ago. It is not really a true crab, but rather the last survivor of an ancient group of creatures whose closest living relatives are the spiders and scorpions.

As perhaps befits a strange creature from the past, the horseshoe crab has four eyes. Atop its shell, on either side of the raised midline, are two. Another pair is set close together along the midline in the very front of the shell.

# MOLLUSKS

All along the coast, on rocks, in the sand and mud, amid the coral, live throngs of incredibly varied creatures that belong to one vast order, the mollusks. This is not to say that you always can see them. Many are buried, or hidden in cracks and crevices. Innumerable others, however, come into view as they go about their lives at the margins of the water. Some of those most likely to be encountered will be described. Others, whose presence is revealed by their beached and often broken shells, will be discussed in a later chapter.

*Using its tail as a prop, a horseshoe crab rights itself after being flipped on its back. Not a true crab but a creature more closely related to spiders than the crustaceans, the horseshoe crab is harmless to man. When on its back, the animal is vulnerable to the predation of gulls. It usually remains in the water unless washed in, but comes high into the littoral region to breed.*

The body of the standard mollusk is soft, with four recognizable divisions. These are the head, a foot, a round mass holding the internal organs, and the mantle which covers it and secretes the limy material of the shell.

The shell may be internal and relatively small, as in the octopus and the giant squid, among the more than 100,000 different kinds of mollusks. Most of them, however, have an external shell. It may be a single unit, as in the snails, or divided into two hinged sections, as in oysters.

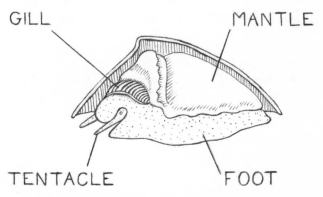

GILL     MANTLE

TENTACLE     FOOT

*Interior anatomy of a typical single-shelled mollusk.*

## CHITONS

One of the most primitive of all mollusks creeps slowly by night over the seaside rocks from New England to Florida. In the day, it retreats to dark corners and cracks. There it appears hardly alive. This creature, the common eastern chiton (*Chaetopleura apiculata*) is less than an inch long. It has a shallow, bowl-like shell over its body. The foot of the mollusk, under the shell, can anchor it to the rock like a suction cup, with incredible firmness.

The shell looks solid when the animal is fastened to the rock. Actually, it is made of eight overlapping plates, which are quite separate. If need be, the chiton can roll up into an armored ball, like a tiny seagoing version of the armadillo.

The chiton feeds by rasping algae off rocks with its rough tongue, or radula. This organ, covered with myriad tiny teeth, is common in mollusks, especially snails.

## SLIPPER SHELLS

There are several snails which may be confused at first glance with the chitons, because all have shells that adhere face down to rocks. The shells, however, are not segmented but in one piece.

Two types called slipper shells are very common on rocks and in the lower tide pools all along the coast. The slipper shells also attach to other mollusks, and to one another. Often, the males fasten themselves to the top of the females. If you see a light-colored shell, about an inch long, bearing a minuscule replica atop it, you have found a female and male eastern white slipper shell (*Crepidula plana*). Slipper shells change sex as they grow, which is why the females always are larger.

Stacked beige-colored slipper shells, more than an inch long, are the common Atlantic species (*C. fornicata*). This is an especially abundant snail. Like other slipper shells, it can move when young but eventually anchors itself permanently. The slipper shell gets its name from the pocket on its underside, that holds the snail's digestive organs. Upside down, the shell with its pocket resembles an open-heeled slipper.

## PERIWINKLES

The most familiar snails at oceanside are the periwinkles. The rough periwinkle mentioned earlier sometimes roams all the way down into the Irish moss and kelp zones. But the lower zones more properly belong to two other kinds. From the rockweed zone down lives the smooth periwinkle (*Littorina obtusata*). Ranging south to the Middle Atlantic states, it has a yellowish shell. Between the realm of the smooth periwinkle, and the zone marked by the rough variety, clusters a third kind. It seems to have come from Europe, probably on the hulls of ships, but is now so abundant north of Maryland it is known as the common periwinkle (*L. littorea*). The shell is dark, and covered with thin spiral lines.

Florida is the home of several very ornate periwinkles. The pricklywinkle (*Nodilittorina tuberculata*), found at the low-tide line, has a shell studded with tiny knobs. The zigzag periwinkle (*L. ziczic*) has a high, pointed shell that is gray to blue, with graceful lines cutting across its spirals. Periwinkles are vegetarians, rasping away algae with their tongues.

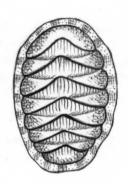

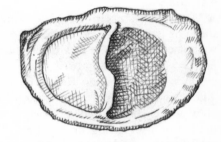

*Common Eastern chiton.*

*Common Atlantic slipper shell.*

*Pricklywinkle.*

# MOON SNAILS, DRILLS, AND DOGWINKLES

Several seaside snails use their tongues to drill through the shells of oysters, clams, mussels, and other fellow mollusks. The Atlantic oyster drill (*Urosalpinx cinerea*) makes a hole that is a perfect circle. Look for it on oyster bars exposed at low tide. Its shell is brown, ribbed, sharply spiraled, and less than an inch long.

The Atlantic dogwinkle (*Nucella lapillus*) feeds largely on blue mussels, after boring through their shells. Its shell is twice the length of the drill's, and more rounded, although with a sharp point. It usually is white, but sometimes brown. Dogwinkles abound on rocks exposed by the tide, especially in New England. South of that, they disappear.

Moon snails (Naticidae) not only drill but also eat through the shells of prey with acid made in a special gland. These are large snails, with shells that sometimes reach the size of a plum. The color is often pearly gray, or blue-gray.

Sandy beaches along the entire coast are the home of moon snails. Their empty shells are washed ashore in droves. Live snails come into view when the tide ebbs. With rare exceptions, they are the largest snails found crawling on the flats. The extra-large foot of the moon snail leaves a wide track as it passes over the wet sand. Even if the snails are not visible, it is a sure sign they are around. So is a low humped area in the damp sand. Beneath it, almost surely, a moon snail is burrowing after clams, its favorite meal.

Most of the sea shells that are found ashore with small, clean holes through them are the remains of mollusks killed by drilling snails. Coastal Indians once used them for jewelry. Do not confuse them with pieces of shells riddled by the boring sponge (*Cliona*). These are so pockmarked by fine holes that the surface of the shell is almost destroyed. The sponge, which does not feed on the shellfish, makes the holes when it encrusts them at one stage in its life.

All of the snails mentioned above produce eggs that can be seen at the edge of the beach. The eggs of the drills and dogwinkles are tiny, almost translucent, packets attached by slender stalks to the walls of crevices, and the bases of Irish moss, rockweed, and other seaweeds. The moon snails lay their eggs within and under a collar they construct by gluing together grains of sand. This is the so-called "sand collar" that often is found on the beach. Once it dries, it is as fragile as ash.

*Washed up on a beach are the signs of the beginning and end of the moon snail's life cycle. The sand collar—a portion of which is pictured here—surrounds the eggs of the snail until they hatch. The empty shell of a moon snail means that its owner has perished. Mollusks do not discard shells as they grow but rather enlarge them.*

## MUD SNAILS

Another group of drilling snails throngs on exposed mud flats. These small brown snails, many only a fraction of an inch long, leave a tracery of deep, narrow trails all over the mud at low tide. Between Maine and Florida live several species of these mud snails, also called by their scientific name, *Nassa*.

When the flats are covered by water, the snails may not be visible. They often hide just below the surface of the mud, with only the tips of their siphons exposed to suck in water for their gills.

Scavengers as well as predators, mud snails have a marvelous sense of smell. The scent of rotting fish or other carrion draws hordes of them and triggers a slow-motion feeding frenzy. Swarming toward their meal, the hungry mud snails even attack and eat one another. Their small dark shells often will completely cover the carcass of a fish stranded on the mud.

## OYSTERS

North of Florida, all the oysters that live near the shore belong to one species, *Crassostrea virginica*, the eastern or American oyster. A different type grows on mangrove roots in Florida, and will be described in another chapter.

Virtually all of the large oysters seen along the shore are female. Small ones, usually less than three inches long, are male. The difference in size stems from the fact that most oysters begin life as males and then change sex.

On hatching, an oyster is a minute oval creature that swims with the swarms of other tiny organisms in the water. Within several days, it begins to assume adult form, and attaches to a surface. It reaches the size at which its sex changes in about three years, and may live to more than six times that long.

## MUSSELS

As mentioned earlier, the blue mussel abounds in the intertidal region at many places between New England and the Carolinas. Two inches long, it can be told by the pretty, blue-black color of its shell, which has growth lines, like the rings of a tree. Another species, the horse mussel (*Modiolus modiolus*) can be seen within the kelp zone along northeastern beaches. Its shell, up to a half foot long, is dark brown.

A few other mussels also may be glimpsed in shallow waters just below the neap-tide line. From Massachusetts south, the inch-long hooked mussel (*Brachidontes recurvus*) colonizes pilings. Its shell has a pronounced curve, growth lines, and is ridged with raised, longitudinal ribs. From North Carolina south, tulip mussels (*M. americanus*) cluster on rocks, shell beds, and similar surfaces. They are the same size as the blue mussel, with a light brown shell. Most colorful of all is the yellow mussel (*B. citrinus*) of southern Florida. It edges into the margins of the shallows, where its narrow yellow shell, about an inch long, can be seen in clear waters.

## COQUINA CLAMS

These small clams (*Donax*), less than a half inch long, share the same habitat as the mole crab, from New Jersey south. They populate the intertidal, following the advance and retreat of the water as they feed. Wedge shaped, the shells of coquina clams are gorgeously colored. They can be white, red, purple, yellow, or orange, in myriad pattern.

Coquina clams may not be readily apparent, although thousands of them may be living underfoot in just a few square feet of sand. The time to look for them is just after a wave has surged up the beach, and is beginning to retreat. The incoming wave can expose so many coquinas that the sand seems to come alive. As soon as they are uncovered they turn up on edge and in a twinkling dig back into the sand. Digging is done by the clam's fleshy foot, protruding through the slightly opened shell. As the clams retreat back into the sand, the retreating wave leaves U-shaped wakes around their tiny shells. They feed while buried, with just their two siphons exposed. Their diet is microorganisms, sucked in with water through one siphon. After the microorganisms are removed the water is eliminated through the other.

## MOSS ANIMALS

Among the animals of the seashore are many that bear a remarkable resemblance to plants, and, indeed, are viewed as such by many people. Some of these animals are among the most primitive of all creatures. Others, known as "moss animals" (Bryozoa), are high on the ladder of life. In fact, scientists who classify animals rate them just a rung or two below the chordates, the group which includes vertebrates, and thus, humans.

Nearly microscopic, the body of a moss animal is wormlike, and ends in a mass of tentacles. Primitive though it may look, the creature has an effective nervous system and a sophisticated digestive apparatus.

Moss animals live in colonies, which take two main forms on the seashore. One is that of an encrustation, often red or white, on shells, rocks, seaweeds, and similar objects. Other moss animals make colonies that have the shape of small trees, and look like fronds of seaweed. These range from just a fraction of an inch to a foot or more long.

Whether crusty or treelike, the colonies consist of myriad animals, each within its own shell. The shell is lidded, so the animal inside can extend its tentacles to feed.

Treelike forms often grow thickly on pilings. The animals of some of the larger colonies are big enough to be seen within the shells, which are transparent. To resolve an encrusted colony into individuals, however, a hand lens is needed.

The moss-animal colony begins with one animal, which then reproduces by budding. As more new animals are formed, the colony either spreads out into a mat or builds branches, depending on the species.


## HYDROIDS

At a glance, it is easy to confuse colonies of moss animals and those of an entirely different group of creatures, the hydroids. Close examination, however, reveals the great differences between them.

Hydroids, along with sea anemones, jellyfish, and corals, are coelenterates, and conglomeration of animals that are among the most simple of all creatures. Their basic form is that of a polyp—a hollow sac, or tube, for digestion, ringed at its mouth by a rim of stinging tentacles, for catching food. There are two basic forms—free-floating, like a jellyfish, and anchored, although not necessarily permanently, like a coral or hydroid. Some undergo both forms, at different stages in their life cycles. Certain hydroids alternate form between generations.

Especially when seen under a lens, the polyp form of the hydroid is clear. Each colony consists of large numbers of them. Like the colonies of moss animals, those of hydroids may look either like encrusted mats, or feathery fronds. Some are several inches long, but most hardly reach an inch. Do not bother to look for them in the sand or mud but on the same sort of surfaces that support moss animal colonies, in tide pools or below low water. One group of hydroids

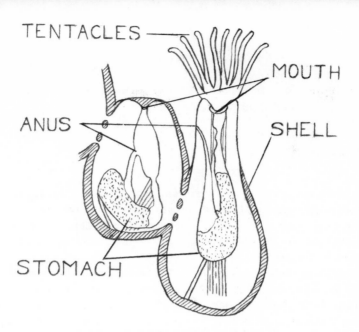

TENTACLES

MOUTH

ANUS

SHELL

STOMACH

*Cross section of a typical bryozoan.*

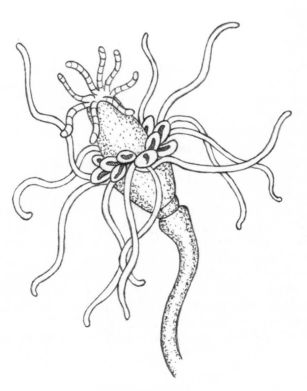

*Typical hydroid.*

lives only on shells tenanted by hermit crabs. The colonies give the shells a pink, fuzzy appearance.

## SEA ANEMONES

Some shells occupied by hermit crabs also provide a holdfast for sea anemones (Actiniaria), the true "flower animals" of the ocean. The sea anemones seen along the shore, generally on rocks, in caves, or in tidepools, are usually only an inch or so high, although much larger ones live in deep water.

The sea anemone has a columnular, muscular body, topped by a ring of petal-like tentacles, and based on a powerful foot. Some species can move from place to place, although slowly. When submerged and feeding, the anemone is fully extended, with tentacles swaying like branches of a tree in the breeze. Those exposed at low tide, however, contract, some so much they almost disappear. In such a state they often escape notice, or at most seem like soft little nubs, or blobs, on the rocks or seaweed.

## CORALS

The very stuff of which the southern coast of Florida is composed was made basically by animals very similar to the sea anemones, although much smaller. These are the true, or stony, corals (Scleractinia). Corals are tiny polyps, in a rainbow of different colors, which form vast colonies. Each member of the colony surrounds itself with a cup of lime, the main building material of the reef.

Coral polyps, minute and delicate, make entire islands. In fact, they are responsible for the largest single structure on earth—the Great Barrier Reef of Australia, which covers 80,000 square miles.

Very sensitive to environmental conditions, reef corals grow only in a narrow belt that girds the planet's midsection. They cannot tolerate temperatures much lower than 68 degrees F. for substantial periods of time. Thus, they do not range much farther north or south than about 25 degrees. The coral reefs of southern Florida, edging slightly above this latitude, are the fringes of the belt. Corals need water that is crystal clear but even then cannot get enough light to live beyond a depth of about 250 feet. Sediment smothers them.

Only when the polyps are dead is coral bleached white. At night,

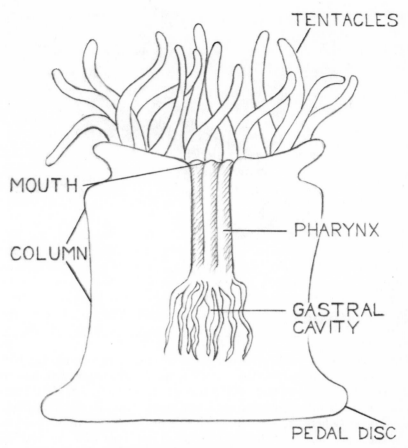

MOUTH

COLUMN

TENTACLES

PHARYNX

GASTRAL
CAVITY

PEDAL DISC

*Cross section of sea anemone.*

under water, the coral takes on its true colors—various reds, greens, yellows, pinks, and browns—as the polyps extend their tentacles to feed.

Living corals form but a thin skin over the bulk of the reef. Below are the remains of billions of organisms which over thousands of years have added to the structure. While corals are the architects and prime builders, they have help. Certain types of algae add a cement of their own. Within the very polyps themselves live other plants, one called "zooxanthellae," which seem to stimulate the production of lime by the corals. Zooxanthellae also use up the polyp's waste and provide it with oxygen in return. Important fabricators of the reef, too, are various worms that build tubes of sand and glue.

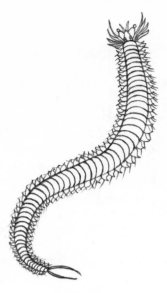

*Clam worm.*

## SEA WORMS

On every sort of seashore, from rocks to reefs, live worms that build tubes in which they live. Most of these worms are segmented, like the terrestrial earthworm, and belong to a grouping known as Polychaeta. Some of their tubes are minuscule, not much larger in diameter than a toothpick. Others are the thickness of a finger. More often than not, the tubes are buried, with only their small openings above the surface. When submerged, however, the worms will extend their bodies from the tubes. Very often the heads of these worms are crowned with feathery projections and tentacles, which give them a flowerlike appearance when projecting from the tube.

Related to the tube worms are the various sandworms and clam worms (*Nereis*) found on almost all types of bottoms, and a favorite bait of fishermen. Bristly, with powerful jaws that can deliver a good pinch, these worms sometimes reach a foot in length. Some of them also build tubes of sand held together with natural glue, but often they range far and wide from their homes. When not swimming, they spend much time in the bottom or under stones.

## SPONGES IN THE SHALLOWS

Several kinds of sponges can be seen at the water's edge, although most inhabit the deeper sea beyond. Usually the shallow-water sponges are low encrustations or lumps on pilings, shells, seaweeds, and rocks. The bright red crusts are red-beard sponges (*Microciona prolifera*), which in deeper water grow "fingers" several inches long. They can be found from the Carolinas north. The boring sponge (*Cliona celata*), destroyer of shellfish, ranges over the same area. It appears as a sulphur-yellow covering of shells, live and dead. New England tidepools are the home of the yellow-green sponge known as the crumb-of-bread (*Halichondria panicea*). Even growing on the shells of rock crabs, it sometimes sprouts stubby little fingers.

All of these sponges belong to a grouping of creatures that is extremely primitive while at the same time remarkable for its survival. Predating most other kinds of animal life, sponges have been around for much more than a half billion years. Only microscopic one-celled animals are more primitive.

Apparently without sensory equipment, and unable to move, sponges gain their living by filtering bits of food from the water. They are remarkably resistant to disease, and possess chemicals—antibiotics—which ward off bacteria. Scientists in a laboratory have put sponges through sieves, only to watch as they reaggregated themselves. Some are colonies, others single animals, but all live in virtually the same way as they did when life was much simpler.

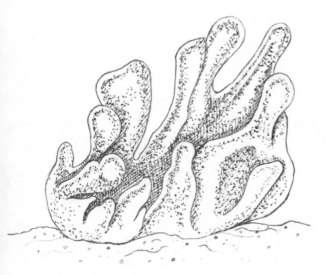

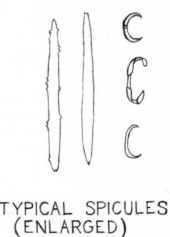

TYPICAL SPICULES
(ENLARGED)

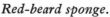

*Red-beard sponge.*

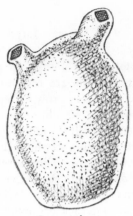

*Sea squirt.*

## SEA SQUIRTS

Clinging to the same type of objects as sponges all along the coast are bulbous, fleshy growths, mostly grape size, that might be mistaken for them. Actually, however, these assorted blobs and nubs are sea squirts (Ascidiacea), which despite their appearance are as high in the scheme of zoological classification as sponges are low.

Sea squirts are chordates, by virtue of the fact that as larvae they have a notochord, the prototype of the backbone. One would never know that sea squirts are ranked so highly from the way they live. Asexual, they spend their time filtering tiny organisms from the water, showing no more activity than a sponge. When disturbed, however, the sea squirt reacts in a way that led to its naming. The creature contracts and jets water from its two siphons.

## SHORE, WATER, AND WADING BIRDS

Birds are the most evident of all animals at the shore. This is true anywhere on the coast, at any season, on the urban waterfront as well as the wild beach. Between Maine and Florida, the variety of bird life ranges from that of the Arctic to the tropics. To know even a portion of the birds belonging to the shore, wading, and water species of the East coast takes considerable patience and study. However, it is not difficult to recognize some general types, and understand something about how they live.

Shorebirds are generally small to moderate size, with relatively long legs, and often long bills. They fly fast, usually in tight flocks, and patrol the beaches afoot, often in large squadrons. Much can be told about how and where they feed by the shape and length of their bills. The ruddy turnstone (*Arenaria interpres*), for example, has a bill that is short and upturned at the tip, for flipping over rocks and gaining access to animals underneath them. The greater yellowlegs (*Totanus melanoleucus*) has a long bill for probing the water and mud. The least sandpiper (*Erolia minutilla*) has a short, slim bill. It pecks at the mud and wet sand, or picks up food from the surface.

Wading birds have very long legs and long, powerful beaks. The largest to be seen with regularity on the coast is the great blue heron (*Ardea herodias*), which stands more than five feet high. Its stiltlike legs enable it to feed beyond the shallows in large bays and lagoons. The middle-size snowy egret (*Leucophoyx thula*) and the common egret (*Casmerodius albus*) feed just off sandy beaches and in the shallows of the larger bays. The small green heron (*Butorides virescens*) hunts in the tidal creeks and very shallow edges of marshes. All the preceding feed by day. The black-crowned night heron (*Nycticorax nycticorax*), on the other hand, hunts after dark. It makes the loud "quonk" that comes from the marshes, and often from the air, in the gathering dusk. The call may help the heron keep in touch in the

FACE PATTERN

*Ruddy turnstone.*

SLIM BILL

YELLOW LEG

*Greater yellowlegs.*

dark. Because of their different hunting territories and habits, several kinds of herons can share the same area without competing with one another.

Most prominent among the water birds are the ducks and geese, and the gulls and terns. Several types of gulls inhabit the coast, but three are especially common over almost all of it. The largest is the great black-backed gull (*Larus marinus*), big as a large hawk, with white underparts and coal-black on its back and the upper side of its wings. It has a heavy hooked bill, and preys on all sorts of sea creatures, as well as young seabirds. Abundant in the North, it spreads to Florida in the winter.

The herring gull (*Larus argentatus*) is somewhat smaller than the greater black-backed species. The wings of the herring gull are gray, darker toward the tips. Similar but still smaller is the ring-billed gull (*Larus delawarensis*). While its body color resembles that of the herring and black-backed gulls, however, it can be distinguished by its yellow legs. As the ring-billed gull's name suggests, it has a small ring on the tip of its bill. Ring-billed gulls are known for their habit of facing the wind when standing on the beach. Dozens of them will stand motionless for minutes at a time, all facing the same direction.

Gulls are both scavengers and predators. Their prey includes shellfish, fish, and the young of other seabirds. Clams are carried aloft and dropped on rocks to break their shells so the gulls can eat their soft bodies. Gulls catch fish not by diving but after alighting on the water.

Terns (Sternidae) dive after fish. This habit and their slim, long wings, make it easy to distinguish them from gulls. When terns, often accompanied by gulls, gather in great numbers over a particular area of the water, it means that the small fish which are their main food are schooling below.

The seasons of migration—autumn and spring—are the best times to see birds at the seashore. Not only are local birds evident, but migrants can be seen passing through or even stopping to rest. This is especially true of shorebirds. Their spring migration is concentrated within a few weeks, as vast numbers hurry to breeding grounds in the Far North. Many have come from as far away as South America.

The shorebirds have a natural clock that schedules them to leave their wintering grounds so they will arrive in the North just after the last snows have gone. This gives them enough time to mate, lay their eggs, and rear their young before the summer ends and the snow returns.

By August, the autumn migration is under way. Because timing is less important at this season, the migration is more dispersed than in

*Black-crowned night herons often roost several miles inland when not foraging at the shore. These birds tolerate people well and even nest in some city parks. Most migrate south from northern shores in the fall but a few stay for the winter.* (Photo: New York Zoological Society)

the spring. First the older birds straggle south. Then, a few weeks later, the young of the year make their first migratory voyage.

Both Canada geese (*Branta canadensis*) and snow geese (*Chen hyperborea*) migrate down the coast in the winter. The majority go no farther south than the Eastern Shore of Delaware, Maryland, and Virginia, where vast grain fields and marshes provide abundant food.

During winter, long lines of dark ducks can be seen flying close to the sea, so low they almost are obscured by the waves. These are white-winged scoters (*Melanitta deglandi*) which live year-round in New England, and winter as far south as the Carolinas. In midautumn, flock after flock, all in line formation, can be seen passing over the sea toward the south.

Cold weather also drives many waterfowl from the north and open sea into bays that are not prone to freezing. This is the time to see brant (*Branta bernicla*) from the mid-Atlantic states north. They resemble small Canada geese without the white cheek markings. Loons (*Gaviidae*), primitive diving birds from ponds in the north woods, spend the winter in bays along the entire coast.

Very few of the shorebirds live all year on any part of the coast. Many of them are seen only in migratory season, although some winter on southern shores. The little sanderling, however, winters along the entire East coast, after breeding in the high Arctic. The sanderling (*Crocethia alba*) is smaller than a robin, with the typical long-legged, slender bill of shorebirds. In winter it is gray above and white below, with dark wings.

Even when snow covers the sand and ice piles up at the water's edge, low tide and bared mud flats will draw small flocks of sanderlings. They scurry about, wading to a depth of about three inches, dipping their heads and poking their bills into the bottom. The holes left by their bills and their tiny footprints cover the flats as the birds search for food. On a silent, wintry beach, they provide a touch of vibrant activity, and a hint of the shorebird squadrons that will arrive in the spring to come.

*White-winged scoter.*

# 4

# *Between the Tides*

For most of the day along almost all of the coast, the littoral, or intertidal, region provides the greatest area for beach exploration. This is untrue only around high tide and on the coral coast, where the tidal range is slight. On sandy shores, the area within the tides corresponds to the middle beach zone. Along rocky coasts, the heart of the littoral is the blurred boundary between the barnacle and rockweed zones, which is the home of hordes of small creatures.

## ISOPODS

Scurrying and hopping among the rockweed and barnacles are pill-shaped animals, many less than an inch long, which resemble insects. Actually, however, they are crustaceans, of a group known as isopods. A multitude of different isopods inhabits the seashore and the waters beyond. Many are scavengers of dead animals. Some are parasites of fish and crabs. Except to specialists, all types look rather alike. A few, however, are noteworthy.

The largest isopod likely to be seen above the Carolinas is a green species, *Idotea baltica*. The males can reach a length of an inch and a half, huge for an isopod. No others found on these shores are of such size. Females of the species, however, are much smaller, often less than an inch long.

If you are probing among the rocks and weeds and see a small mote roll into a little ball, you have found another isopod, *Sphaeroma quadridentatum*. Light-colored, less than a half inch long, it is the only isopod with this habit of curling up when disturbed, in the fashion of a hedgehog. The species ranges along all of the coast, chiefly among the rocks, except for southern Florida.

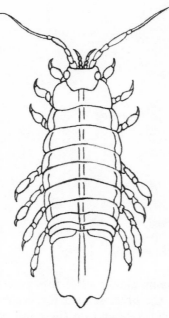

Idotea baltica.

## TIDEPOOL INSECTS

Creeping about the barnacles, or massing in great numbers on the surfaces of tidepools, even water-filled crevices, is the seashore's most unusual insect, *Anurida maritima*. A scavenger, this creature is known as
the "tidepool insect," because of the habitat in which it is most conspicuous. Great numbers of these insects, looking for all the world like
iron filings drawn together by a magnet, cluster on the water of the
pools. Often the masses are so densely packed they appear to be a solid
blue-gray film. Only if disturbed—say, by an inquisitive finger—do
they break up into individual specks.

The tidepool insect has a soft body about an eighth-inch long. It is
covered with a coat of fine, dark hair, which traps air bubbles. This
provides an air supply for the insect to breathe when it dives, and
gives it buoyancy when afloat.

*Anurida maritima* belongs to an old and distinguished line of insects,
the springtails. Among the most primitive of all insects, springtails live
from pole to pole. Often their homes are so harsh no other insects—or
any other creatures, for that matter—can survive there. Springtails,
for instance, jump about the polar snows and high on peaks such as
Mount Everest. In keeping with this tradition, the tidepool insect is
one of the few to live in salt water.

# ROVING DOGWINKLES

Dogwinkles of the same type seen at the water's edge also rove through the barnacles. The snails are especially thick in the barnacle patches that are shielded from the direct surf. As far as the barnacles are concerned, the dogwinkles are unwelcome, for their purpose in visiting the barnacle zone is predation. Dogwinkles prey on barnacles as well as shellfish.

The dogwinkle does not attack the barnacle in the same way as it gains access to the meat of a mussel. Instead of drilling through the barnacle shell, the dogwinkle literally shoves its foot into the door. The snail's muscular foot is strong enough to pry open the lid to the barnacle's fortress.

If the dogwinkles encountered among the barnacles look larger than those down below, it is not by chance. Not until they near a half inch in length do they begin to climb toward the middle of the littoral and seek barnacles as prey.

# TRAVELING LIMPETS

North of New Jersey, the rockweed forest is the home of a primitive snail known as the Atlantic plate limpet (*Acmaea testudinalis*). It might be mistaken for a slipper shell or chiton, because it has a bowl-shaped shell that lies face down on the rock. The limpet's shell, however, has a pronounced peak. Some limpets, in fact, have shells that are sharply cone-shaped. The shells are blue to brown in color, with lines radiating from the high point to the edge.

When the rocks are above water, the limpet sticks fast to the rock and does not move. In this case, however, appearances are deceiving. If you could watch a limpet after it was covered by water, you might see it slide here and there over the rock, propelled by its foot, as it feeds. Limpets, like periwinkles, eat algae scraped from the rocks with their sandpapery tongues. They are especially active when the tide rises at night.

The Atlantic plate limpet is a cold-water creature. It is found no farther south than New York. On middle Atlantic and southern shores, the limpet is replaced by related but somewhat different animals called keyhole limpets. Common from New Jersey south is the cayenne keyhole limpet (*Dindora cayensis*). Its ridged, dark gray shell has a hole at its apex, a trait of all the keyhole limpets which gives them their name. Water that passes under the shell and over the animal's gills as it respires is expelled through the hole. So is waste.

*Keyhole limpet.*

## JELLYFISH

The littoral of sandy shores is the place where one is most likely to come across jellyfish stranded by the surf. Before anything else is said about jellyfish, a warning is in order. The stinging cells of even a dead jellyfish can be active for some time after beaching. Although excessive fear is foolish, it is wise to be cautious about these creatures. The best advice is the old saw, "Look, but don't touch."

Without the support of water, the body of a jellyfish is an oozy glob, giving no hint of the immense grace it has in the sea. Less than 5 percent of the body is composed of solids. The rest is water, making the jellyfish almost one with the medium it inhabits. The jelly, however, has a firm if soft consistency, and jellyfish are not nearly as delicate as they appear. They even have survived frozen in ice.

The jellyfish found in our waters range in size from true giants to minims with a body, or "bell," less than a half inch in diameter. The monster of them all is the pink, or Arctic, jellyfish, *Cyanea capillata*, also known as the lion's mane. In Arctic and sub-Arctic waters, where it prospers, this great reddish-pink jellyfish can reach a diameter of eight feet, trailing hundreds of tentacles for up to two hundred feet in the water.

Arctic jellyfish of such size are rare along our coasts, and indeed, few of any size are found south of New Jersey. Most of those in our waters are a foot or so across, at most. Normally, the Arctic jellyfish retreats northward with the coming of summer. By July, few remain south of Maine. Exceptionally cool spring weather, however, can cause the jellyfish to linger, sometimes in immense numbers.

This occurred in the spring and early summer of 1978. Vast shoals of jellyfish clogged the water near the beaches of Connecticut and New York. At one point the eastern end of Long Island Sound contained assemblages of jellyfish covering several square miles of surface. The jellyfish were so dense that they were spaced just inches apart in a layer a yard deep. The water took on a red tinge from their bodies.

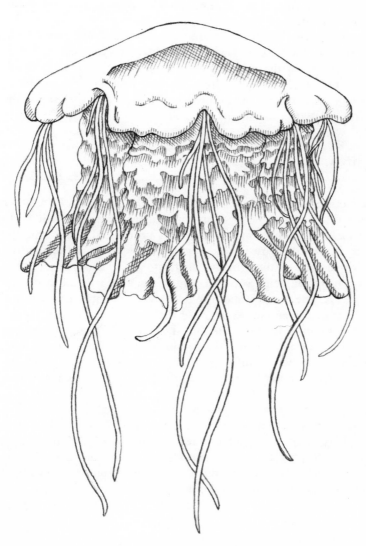

*Arctic jellyfish.*

Naturally, large numbers of *Cyanea* were washed ashore. Beaches in many areas were repeatedly closed until the warm summer weather set in and the jellyfish invasion ceased. The stinging cells in the tentacles of *Cyanea* are capable of inflicting severe pain, especially in people sensitive to the poison.

*Cyanea* is the only jellyfish of its color likely to be found on our coast. If you find a white jellyfish, with a bell up to the diameter of a dinner plate, it is another common species, the moon jelly (*Aurelia aurita*). It is not considered dangerous. White to milk-yellow, the bell of the moon jelly contains four prominent sexual organs, shaped like horseshoes or rings, and arranged around its centerpoint. Those of the male are pink, easy to see, while the female's sexual organs are white and blend into the general color of the body.

Unlike the Arctic jellyfish, the moon jelly does not have long, trailing tentacles. Its tentacles are short, little more than a fringe around its edge. Long or short, however, the tentacles of all jellyfish do the same job—trap prey, sting it to death or insensibility, and bring it to their mouths. The size of the prey varies according to that of the jellyfish, from plankton to rather large fish.

# MAN-OF-WAR

The same tactic is employed to snare prey by the man-of-war, another coelenterate often found washed up on beaches, and mistaken for a jellyfish. Common mainly on the southern portion of the coast, the man-of-war is identified by its iridescent blue float, or air bag, often crested with an edge of pink. From this float, which can be more than a foot long, hang tentacles, some of which can reach a length of one hundred feet. As the wind pushes the float over the surface of the sea, the tentacles snag fish and other prey for the man-of-war to eat.

During the summer months, the sand beaches of Florida sometimes are dotted with the man-of-war, borne in by the waves. Leave them alone. The sting of the man-of-war is very dangerous. It can cause intense pain, welts, vomiting, paralysis, and even in a few extreme cases, death.

Despite its superficial resemblance to the jellyfish, the man-of-war is very different. It is not an individual animal, like the jellyfish, but in reality a colony of many small polyps, individuals of different types that carry on distinct tasks for the survival of the group. One type of polyp, for instance, creates the float, others are hunters, while still others consume and digest the food used by the colony.

*A dead man-of-war has drifted up onto a beach at Fort Lauderdale, Florida. Even though not alive, it still may inflict a serious sting to someone who touches it. The dark spots on the sand are oil that has washed ashore.*

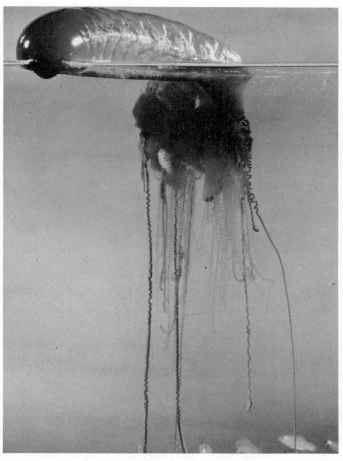

*Most common in warmer waters, the man-of-war sometimes drifts as far north as New England in the summer. It is to be avoided.*
(Photo: Miami Seaquarium)

## STAR CORAL

The presence of those other well-known coelenterates, the corals, is expected on beaches in Florida, but it often comes as a surprise to people who find them as far north as southern New England. Occasionally, strollers and beachcombers on northern beaches turn up small fragments of what at first glance appear to be stone, but on inspection prove to be true coral.

The type of coral involved is star coral (*Astrangia danae*), which grows just offshore in small colonies only a few inches across. Living star coral is light pink. The tiny chunks that are found on the beach are dirty white. The coral gets its name from the cups formed by the polyps, which are rayed, like stars. These are easily visible on stranded pieces, which have the feel of rough stones.

Occasionally, true tropical corals are stranded on the beaches just south of Cape Lookout, North Carolina. These are not brought up from down Florida way, but instead come from just offshore. The flat, sandy bottom is studded with small coral formations called "heads," which from Florida south do not grow alone but on the landward side of coral reefs.

*A chunk of dead star coral on a beach is clearly marked with the cuplike shelters of the polyps that formed it. Star coral is made up of small polyp colonies, numbering less than three dozen individuals each.*

# SEA STARS AND SEA URCHINS

Clinging to the wet boulders and nestling in the crevices of the rocky littoral can be seen sea stars and sea urchins, prickly-skinned relatives belonging to the phylum of echinoderms. The name echinoderm is particularly descriptive, because it is taken from Greek words meaning "spiny skin." Both the sea stars and sea urchins are studded with spines. This is especially true of the latter, some of which bear spines several inches long.

These long-spined sea urchins (*Diadema*) are dark brown-black and extend northward into Florida waters, most often found on reefs. More typical of the urchins living on our coast, from Cape Cod south, is the purple sea urchin (*Arbacia punctulata*). About the size of a golf ball, with short, stubby spines, it is found on littoral rocks, as well as in deep water. In crevices purple sea urchins sometimes cluster by the scores. They graze on algae, and eat many kinds of animal matter, dead and alive.

From New Jersey north lives the green sea urchin (*Strongylocentrotus droebachiensis*). It thrives in the rockweed jungle, and in tide pools. Along the southern third of the coast, beginning in North Carolina, can be found the rock-boring sea urchin (*Echinometra subangularis*). It and the green urchin are about the same size as the purple species. The rock-boring urchin has greenish spines tipped with purple.

The spines of the urchin are mounted individually on a shell, round above and flat below, and known as a "test." It holds the internal organs, the bulk of which are devoted to reproduction. The urchin can be a veritable egg machine. A single female can produce millions of eggs at one time.

The fertilized egg of an urchin, and of other echinoderms, for that matter, becomes an embryo that is rather remarkable. The reason is that it bears a strong resemblance to the early stages of embryonic chordates—the phylum that includes vertebrates, and thus, humans. Embryonic urchins, in fact, have the beginnings of a backbone. This oddity, and the abundance of eggs urchins produce, makes these animals extremely important in embryological studies—for instance, to test the effects of various chemicals on the developing embryo.

As it develops, however, the echinoderm embryo undergoes marked change. In the beginning, it is bilaterally symmetrical, like all of the animals except protozoa, sponges, and coelenterates. Before adulthood, however, urchins and other echinoderms take on radial symmetry, like a jellyfish.

*Lying on the sands of southern Florida, this test of a sea urchin has lost most of its spines. The test shows the radial symmetry of the echinoderms. The bulk of the urchin's body, within the test of a live specimen, consists of reproductive organs.*

A close look at a sea urchin shows the basic pattern on which echinoderms are built. Besides being radial, it has tube feet interspersed among its spines. The feet can be extended and end in powerful suction cups. Urchins cling to the rocks and travel by means of these feet, and also their spines, which are movable.

Underneath, in the exact center of the urchin's body, is its mouth, surrounded by five white teeth. The mouth is the visible part of a muscular internal structure called Aristotle's lantern, after its discoverer and the fact that it resembles an ancient oil lamp.

When an urchin dies, the spines fall out of their sockets on the test, and the animal's soft parts disappear. The skeleton of the lantern remains, however, inside the shell. Dried urchin tests often are washed up on the littoral of sandy beaches, although the living animals seldom are found there.

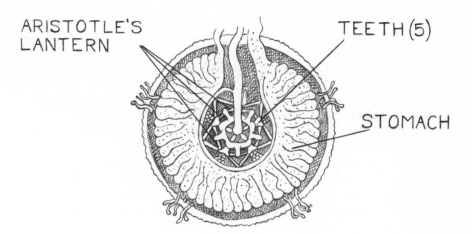

ARISTOTLE'S LANTERN

TEETH (5)

STOMACH

*Underside of sea urchin showing Aristotle's lantern.*

*Upside down, this sea urchin reveals its mouth with its five pointed teeth and the circular structure known as Aristotle's lantern. Muscles surrounding the "lantern" can extend the teeth. The gills of the animal also are arranged around the lantern.*

Dead sea stars (incorrectly called starfish) also wash up on the sand. Among the numerous sea stars along our coast, many live on sandy bottoms. Most of these are common only in water that is deep—sometimes several thousand feet. To see live sea stars, the best place to look is among the rocks of the intertidal, or on pilings exposed as the tide lowers.

Three species are common on the intertidal rocks. One of these is so abundant it is known as the common sea star (*Asterias forbesi*). It exists all along the coast, although only rarely in northern New England. Sometimes almost a foot in diameter, it comes in a wide range of colors, from gray to purple. A sure way to identify it, however, is to look for a spot of very bright orange on its top side, slightly off center. The mark is called a "madreporite," and is a sieve through which water enters a system of canals in the sea star's body.

The canals lead to the tube feet. Such a system is characteristic of the echinoderms as a group, and is the key to the way these animals extend their feet. This is accomplished when the sea star or other echinoderm squeezes the water in the canals by muscular action, pushing the feet to their full length.

The tube feet of the sea star are on its underside only, unlike those of the urchin, which cover the test. On the arms of the sea star, the feet are a deadly weapon against oysters, clams, and other mollusks. The sea star wraps its arms around the shellfish, and anchors its feet to both halves of the shell. Applying tremendous suction, the sea star steadily pulls the shells apart until the shellfish is exhausted and a gap appears. Then the sea star extrudes its stomach out of its mouth and into the open shell, where the shellfish is digested.

Sea stars are thus the bane of oystermen, who used to destroy the animals by ripping them in pieces—that is, until it was discovered the sea stars can regenerate themselves. The animal not only can replace lost arms, but sometimes an arm will grow an entirely new sea star to replace its lost owner.

North of Cape Cod, the common sea star mixes with and eventually is all but replaced by a close relative, the purple sea star (*A. vulgaris*). The two types are difficult to tell apart by general body color. However, the madreporite of the purple sea star is light yellow, rather than brilliant orange, as in its cousin. Occasionally, a few purple sea stars can be found as far south as North Carolina, but it generally is a northern animal. The same is true of the blood sea stars (*Henricia*). Colored as its name implies, the blood sea star at its largest will fit into the palm of one's hand. It clings to the depths of crevices and nestles in deep corners of tide pools.

Along the coast of Florida, a really spectacular sea star may be en-

*Sea Star.*

countered. It is the giant sea star (*Oreaster reticulatus*), sometimes more than a foot and a half across. Yellowish, it inhabits the sandy bottoms of the shallows, but where tidal range is small and flats stretch out beyond the shore, sometimes ventures into the intertidal. This animal lives in offshore shallows as far north as the Carolinas, although it is seldom seen alive on beaches there.

## SAND DOLLARS

Another echinoderm of the sandy bottoms is the sand dollar, which resembles a sea urchin covered with minute, very soft spines, and flattened to a thin pancake. Hard to see in the water, the sand dollar, or more correctly its test, is often brought ashore and tossed up on the littoral.

*The sand dollar—a dead specimen is shown here—is another echino-derm with the group's typical radial symmetry. When echinoderms are in the larval stage, however, they have bilateral symmetry, like the vertebrates.*

The sand-dollar test is hard to mistake for something else. It is bleached white and on its upper surface carries a marking resembling a five-rayed star. This is the emblem of the echinoderms, whose radial body plan is built on a basic five-rayed pattern.

In New England, there are two sand dollars, the common (*Echinarachnius parma*), and the type known as the keyhole urchin (*Mellita testudinata*), which ranges all the way south as well.

Sand dollars are but part of the beachcomber's treasure trove tossed up by the waves onto the littoral. As a rule shells and other items are lost in holes and crevices, or smashed to bits if washed against a rocky shore. On the sandy intertidal stretches, they are strewn about in plain view. So varied are these leavings of the sea along our sandy coasts that many books, such as specialty guides to seashells or marine algae, are needed to mention even a sizable portion of them. However, some of those likely to be encountered on a casual beach walk will be described here.

# WHELKS, KNOBBED AND CHANNELED

Of all large snail shells found on the coast, the most common have to be those of the big whelks, the knobbed (*Busycon carica*) and the channeled (*B. canaliculata*) species. These whelks, also called conchs, rove the bottoms just offshore searching for clams to eat. The whelks open the clam by brute strength, prying apart the two sides of the shell with a strong, muscular foot.

The two whelks have shells that are somewhat similar. Both are capped by pronounced whorls, and are roughly the shape of a pear, five to eight inches long, with a wide aperture. However, the species are easy to tell apart. The aperture of the knobbed whelk is cream to brick red in color, that of the channeled whelk, brown.

The key difference, though, is in the design of the whorls. As the names of the species suggest, the whorls of one are crowned by prominent knobs, the other heavily channeled, or grooved.

Both whelks range from Cape Cod south, to Georgia in the case of the knobbed whelk, and into Florida for the channeled type. In some areas where these giant snails are especially common, such as along the sea islands of Georgia, their shells litter the beaches.

*An old knobbed whelk shell, worn by the waves, lies on the beach. The knobbed whelk, which can reach nine inches in length, is the biggest whelk on the Atlantic coast. The channeled whelk, inhabiting similar waters, is almost as large.*

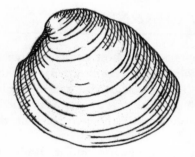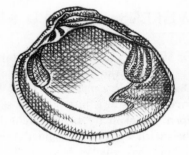

*Northern quahog.*

## SURF CLAMS AND QUAHOGS

Largest of the many types of clamshells found on the East coast is the surf clam (*Spisula solidissima*), which lives as far south as South Carolina. It can grow up to ten inches long, has a very solid shell, white to cream-colored, and marked with strong concentric lines, indicating growth. The living clams inhabit the sandy bottoms from the lower edge of the intertidal to a depth of one hundred feet.

The surf clam is prized as an edible species. So is another type of large clam whose shells are scattered along the sands all the way to Florida. This is the northern quahog (*Mercenaria mercenaria*), or hard-shelled clam. Small ones are known as littleneck or cherrystone. The shell is thick and heavy, with growth ridges, grayish outside and white, edged by purple, within. It inhabits muddy bottoms, especially in bays.

## SOFT-SHELLS, RAZORS, AND OTHER CLAMS

Elongate white clamshells, tinged with gray and dark gray inside, belong to the soft-shell, or steamer clam (*Mya arenaria*). It inhabits mixed bottoms of mud and sand, where it hides below the surface with siphon tube protruding into the water. The siphoning system sucks in water from which the clam filters organic particles and small animals as food. Then the water is expelled through the same tube, which contains both ingoing and outgoing conduits.

From New England to Carolina, the range of the soft-shell, this clam often invades the intertidal. When the tide is in, the clam extends its siphon, but withdraws it when the littoral is uncovered. If these clams feel the vibrations of footsteps on the exposed beach, they burrow deeper, releasing a jet of water above the sand.

Long narrow clamshells resembling the handles of straight razors or jackknives frequently turn up on the beach. These belong to several species, longest of which is the half-foot Atlantic razor, or jackknife, as you will. Its scientific name is *Ensis directus*. The shell is brown outside and violet within. It is most often found where the bottom is mud mixed with sand, and lives as far south as the Carolinas. Large numbers of these clams inhabit the shallows, just below low water. They seldom are seen alive, however, because they are highly sensitive to disturbance of the sand, and dig with amazing rapidity.

Among the other long-shelled clams is the stout razor (*Tagelus*) with a blunt-ended, strongly rectangular shell about four inches long. Found from Cape Cod south, this clam is a burrower in the mud. Like the Atlantic razor, it digs rapidly. Its shell is green-brown on the external surface, blue inside.

From Virginia south live the semele clams (*Semele*). Their shells are small, seldom more than than an inch long, and have a pronounced roundness to their shape. The white semele (*S. proficua*) is white outside, while its interior is shiny yellow. The purple semele (*S. purpurascens*) has an orange to purple interior, while its shell can vary in color across the board. Running over its shell, however, are an uneven series of rays. A related clam, *Cumingia tellinoides*, leaves snow-white, thin shells only a half inch long on beaches as far north as Cape Cod.

Especially along the southern half of the coast, the very attractive shells of clams called arks are commonly swirled in to the intertidal sands. These shells are white, with a graceful, rounded dome shape, and are strongly ribbed. They also are told by their extreme sturdiness, even in small ones, and the teeth on the shell's hinge. Typical of them is the ponderous ark (*Noetia ponderosa*). It is three inches across, and its ribs are strong enough to be easily counted. There are between twenty-seven and thirty-one of them. The ponderous ark, rare in the North, is abundant from Maryland south. Like most other arks, it inhabits the sandy shallows and when alive is covered with a dark brown growth.

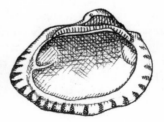

*Ponderous ark.*

The true jewel of Atlantic clamshells can be picked up on almost any sand beach, but it is so small—about the size of a pencil eraser—it often escapes notice. This shell is that of the amethyst gem clam (*Gemma gemma*). Very shiny, almost as though polished, it is beige touched with purple and red on the outside, and white and purple within.

## BLACKENED OYSTER SHELLS

On many ocean beaches, there is a litter of oystershells, many far from the water's edge, which are black-colored, often entirely so. The coloration comes from burial for long years in the muck of a salt marsh. Oysters grow mainly in bays, lagoons, and marshes, and as the animals die their shells accumulate in the mud below, where they are stained and blackened. Somehow, the shells are disinterred—perhaps by dredging, or naturally by a storm, and swept out to sea, then carried in to the beach. On barrier beaches, the shells are often unearthed as the barriers are pushed landward over the sites of old bays and marshes, a process described earlier in the case of Assateague Island. If you see blackened oystershells on a barrier, the chances are it stands on what once was an old salt marsh.

## SCALLOPS

Few seashells are more identifiable than that of the scallop, which for years has been the symbol of a major oil company. Just as the name says, the shell is scalloped, around its edge. Fan-shaped, the shell is ridged by pronounced ribs—approximately eighteen in the common Atlantic bay scallop (*Aequipecten irradians*), which lives from Georgia north. A dweller of the shallows, the bay scallop is the basis of a major shellfish industry, especially in New England, where it is abundant. It displays the traits which makes all of the scallops, worldwide, extraordinary among shellfish.

In the first place, the bay scallop has eyes—up to forty of them, gorgeous blue organs which, when a live animal opens its shell, can be seen peeping from within. Secondly, the scallop swims like a rocket. Propulsion comes from water jetted out of the scallop as it clamps the two halves, or valves, of its shell together. Each time the shellfish performs this action, it hurtles for several feet, the direction determined by the angle at which the scallop purposely expels the water jet.

Most scallops like one another's company, so they live in large beds. The beds of the bay scallops are just offshore or even in the tidal areas of rivers. Bay scallop shells, usually dirty brown in color, are about three inches across. Sometimes scallop shells more than twice that size are washed ashore. These belong to the Atlantic deep-sea species (*Placopecten magellanicus*), which often inhabits bottoms several hundred feet down. A variety of small scallops, only an inch or two in diameter, can be found on southern beaches: The calico scallop (*Aequipecten gibbus*) can be brown, white, or yellow, flecked with calico markings. The sentis scallop (*Chlamys sentis*) is orange or orange mixed with white.

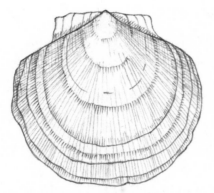

*Atlantic deep-sea scallop.*

# BORERS

Two of the most ornate clamlike shells which can be seen on the beach belong to mollusks which have the ability to bore holes in clay, peat, and even cement and rock. Distributed all along the coastline is the false angel wing (*Petricola pholadiformis*), an elongate white shell about two inches long, with rough ribs. The true angel wing (*Cyrtopleura costata*), really common only south of New York, is white, delicate, ridged, and about five inches long. These creatures dwell mostly in marshes and mud flats but wash up on nearby sand beaches. Incredibly, these shellfish burrow into the hardest of surfaces, causing shorelines, sea walls, and pilings to crumble. They are among a motley group of animals known collectively as the marine borers, and responsible for millions of dollars of damage to seaside structures each year.

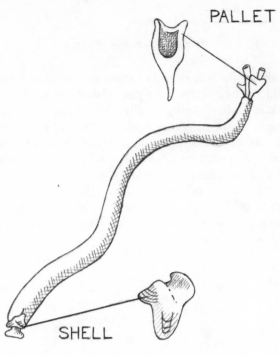

*Shipworm.*

## RIDDLED WOOD—WORK OF THE BORERS

The existence of many marine borers is evident on the beach not so much by their presence but by the stranded chunks of wood riddled with their burrows. Although the creatures themselves may not be in the wood, it is possible to guess at their identity by the character of the holes they make.

Rounded burrows, as though made by a bit an inch or so in diameter, are the work of a clamlike mollusk known as *Martesia*. The burrows are seldom more than two and a half inches long. Holes of similar diameter, but several inches, or even a yard long, are bored by queer mollusks called shipworms (*Teredo* and *Bankia*). These ugly creatures do indeed resemble long, slimy worms. Their shells are reduced to small boring devices set at their rear ends.

Several crustaceans also are among the borer population. One is *Limnoria*, an isopod resembling an ordinary woodlouse. Another is the amphipod *Chelura terebrans*. Both of these small creatures leave an interwoven tracery of very fine burrows, about a twentieth of an inch in diameter. Despite their size, these borers like all of the others are immensely destructive. A pack of them can reduce a piling fourteen inches in diameter to wreckage in less than a year.

# GOOSE BARNACLES

Freshly beached chunks of driftwood may carry clumps of odd creatures resembling fan-shaped barnacles on fleshy stalks. That is exactly what they are. More precisely, they are goose barnacles (*Lepas*), a type which prefers attachment to floating objects.

Goose barnacles may stay whole for some hours after they are beached, if shorebirds or other predators do not get them. Some of their shells are quite large, up to two inches long, and they often are partly open, giving the curious a good view of what a barnacle really looks like. Even a casual examination of a beached goose barnacle can reveal its featherlike feet curling from the shell's opening. By prying apart the shell, we can expose the entire body of the crustacean within.

# STRANDED SEAWEEDS

Whether the shore is sandy, rocky, muddy, or marshy, seaweeds left by the waves will be draped upon it. Some of these plants are readily identifiable as those demarking the zones of the rocky shore—kelp, Irish moss, and rockweed. These plants frequently are ripped from their holdfasts by the surf and washed ashore. With them often comes sea lettuce (*Ulva*). It grows in broad, thin sheets, very shiny, green and up to a yard long. Similar to sea lettuce but purple is sea laver (*Porphyra*).

Long green strands, resembling curly grass but like all true seaweeds really algae, belong to *Enteromorpha*, sometimes called "intestine seaweed." Another green seaweed, *Codium*, can be mistaken for sponge, which has a similar consistency and look. *Codium* grows in thick, tubular branches and is treelike in shape unless broken into pieces. Globs of what appear to be red jelly on the beach often turn out to be a seaweed called *Dasya*. In the water, it has an entirely different appearance for it spreads out fine, graceful fronds, sometimes more than two feet long.

From time to time in the North, and often in the South, the waves bring in a light brown seaweed with air bladders and fronds separated into small blades. This is *Sargassum*, and sometimes it travels a long way to the shore. *Sargassum* floats with its air bladders on the surface of the sea, often gathering in large masses. The most famous of these covers an immense area in the mid-Atlantic south of Bermuda, known as the Sargasso Sea.

*Attached to a timber, these goose barnacles were washed ashore on a southern Florida beach. The barnacles were still wet and alive but unless the timber was carried back to sea, they died not long after the photo was taken. Goose barnacles often attach to floating and moving objects on the ocean. They are found on both whales and ships.*

A mass of floating *Sargassum* has its own specialized community of animals, many of which have natural camouflage that matches the weeds. Among them is the sargassum fish (*Histrio histrio*), which is trimmed with tabs and filaments of skin that resemble the fronds of the plants. It even climbs through the *Sargassum* tangle with its mobile fins.

## THE STRAND LINE

The upper boundary of the intertidal beach is delineated by a windrow of stranded plants—seaweeds, eelgrass, and often marsh grasses washed in by the highest tides. The lineal quality of this "strand line," as noted earlier, is most obvious on broad, sandy beaches. Among the boulders and in the back reaches of marshes, the line is broken into isolated clumps and heaps, but these also mark the farthest progression of the tides.

Entangled in the beached plants is a conglomeration of just about every item the sea leaves on shore, such as feathers, dead fish, sponges, and the shells described previously. Most of the materials that are lightweight, and easily carried by waves or whisked by the wind, ultimately end up in the strand line. Noteworthy are the egg cases of marine animals.

## WHELK CASES

Laid in long strings, the egg cases of the large whelks are especially eye catching. The cases are circular sand-colored capsules, about the size of a nickel, each attached at one end to a cord that can be several inches long. Often such strings consist of dozens of capsules. Dried and enmeshed in the strand line, the strings will rustle softly in the sea breeze.

The capsules differ slightly according to species. That of the knobbed whelk, for example, has a thick edge, rather like a coin. The capsule of the channeled whelk has a thin margin, almost knife edged. Each capsule is capable of holding up to one hundred eggs. The strings are attached by the female whelk to an underwater holdfast, like a stone.

## MERMAID'S PURSE

The egg case of skates (Rajidae) is commonly called the "mermaid's purse." A black, rectangular packet, the case does resemble a small wallet, except for the hornlike projections that curve from each of its four corners. When the egg case leaves the female skate, the horns are coated with a gum that anchors the packet in place until the embryonic fish within hatches.

Skates are relatively small, harmless relatives of the sharks, and the rays, and like the latter are pancake flat, with a long tail and broad pectoral fins that flap like wings when the fish swims. Most skates off our shores are about the size of a large frypan.

The embryo within the egg case soon grows much larger than its nursery. However, the little skate remains in a rolled-up position, looking like a crepe, until it hatches. When the fish is ready to hatch the case splits down a seam—the break is visible on the empty cases— and the youngster wriggles out. Quickly the fish unrolls and swims away.

## BITS AND PIECES

Virtually every heap of stranded vegetation holds countless bits and pieces of marine creatures—the bones, even vertebrae, of fish, for instance, the cast-off shells of crabs, and sometimes of lobsters. The presence of the empty shells of these crustaceans does not necessarily mean that they have died. On the contrary, the shells may indicate their former owners are prospering.

Crabs, lobsters, and their relatives shed their shells—or more properly, exoskeletons—as they grow. After shedding, or "molting," the body of the crustacean is soft and vulnerable. But a new shell quickly grows to accommodate the creature's increased bulk.

## LOBSTERS

Molting is intimately tied to the reproduction of the American lobster (*Homarus americanus*), abundant in northern waters but ranging in lesser numbers all the way to North Carolina. Young lobsters molt several times annually, as their growth is rapid. Adults, however, go

*Delicately speckled with sand, a "mermaid's purse," the egg case of a skate, has been washed ashore. A single skate embryo develops in the purse, which is anchored to the bottom or an undersea object by a sticky substance on its horns. When the young skate is ready to hatch, the egg case splits at the end between the horns opposite those which are glued in place.*

for long periods without changing shells. Two years is typical for a female. The female lobster can only mate within a day or so of shedding. This means that the older and larger a female grows, the less she mates. At the same time, however, the number of eggs produced at one time increases, up to more than fifty thousand for a pot-sized animal.

South of North Carolina, the lobster-shell fragments found on the beach belong to a totally different species from the heavy-clawed type to the north. The southern variety is the spiny lobster (*Panulirus argus*), sometimes incorrectly called a "crayfish." It has extra-long antennae but is without large claws. Its meat is mainly in the tail. Under water, on reefs and among rocks, spiny lobsters are particularly vocal. When disturbed they emit a loud series of staccato clicks, or at least that is how human ears hear it.

## SEA BEANS

Among the flotsam and jetsam occasionally there is a piece of something that obviously comes from far, far away, and thus evokes images of distant shores and exotic places. In this category falls a varied assortment of seeds and nuts from tropical America that continually wash up on the shores of south Florida, particularly the Keys. Among these "sea beans," as they are called locally, are Brazil nuts, tropical almonds, palm nuts, and others that have hard, rot-resistant shells. Fallen from faraway trees directly into the sea, or washed there by rivers, the sea beans are carried by currents through the Caribbean to the coast of North America, where they are sought after by beachcombers.

## SAND HOPPERS

Especially at night, the strand line attracts hordes of half-inch crustaceans called sand hoppers, which feed on decaying seaweed, and occasionally animal matter. Also known as "beach fleas," an incorrect designation, they swarm among the weeds, creeping and jumping with abandon. Common on sandy beaches all along the coast is the species *Orchestia agilis*, which is brown or green in color. It might be mistaken for an isopod, but its body is shrimplike, rather than flattened. When not foraging, the sand hopper lives in a tiny burrow which it excavates just above the high tide mark. The burrows sometimes can be seen, and are about as wide as a pencil.

# OF LAND AND SEA

Although it lives most of the time on land, the sand hopper is a creature of the sea. It has gills and cannot breathe in dry surroundings. It finds plenty of dampness in the seaweed and under the sand. At the same time, the sand hopper also has many traits of a land animal. It typifies the creatures that are to be found at the upper portions of the littoral. Some are marine animals making do on land—like the ghost crab to be described in the next chapter. Others are land animals come to the edge of the sea for food. Ladybird and tiger beetles rove the strand. Flickers on autumn migration along the coast stop to probe for the insects and other small animals. At night raccoons, skunks, foxes, and deer visit the beach to see what the sea has brought them.

Above the strand line, the true land world begins. The sea, however, does not relinquish all its influence. Some of its creatures, as the next chapter explains, venture well beyond the intertidal, to mix with those of the land among plants that, while typically of seaside varieties, are truly terrestrial.

# 5

## *Behind the Beach*

Just above the strand line on broad, sandy beaches south of New Jersey, small holes usually can be seen at the base of the dunes. The holes are up to two inches in diameter and often are fronted with small piles of loose sand, marked by scratchy tracks. The creatures that dig the holes and inhabit them, seldom are seen in the daylight, except sometimes when the sky is badly overcast. At night, however, the hole dwellers emerge, often in such numbers that the beach is literally crawling with them. They are ghost crabs (*Ocypode quadrata*), creatures with rather square bodies a few inches across at the biggest. The name is exceptionally fitting, and not just because of the way the crabs rove nocturnally. Ghost crabs are natural will-o'-the-wisps, seeming to appear and disappear as they wish. This ability reflects natural camouflage at its best. The ghost crab matches the color of the sand so perfectly it is almost impossible to detect if it is motionless, its response when alarmed.

Under the cover of night, the crabs are safe from gulls and other diurnal birds which may prey on them. Once darkness mantles the seaside, hordes of crabs skitter about in search of dead animal matter, smaller creatures, and other things to eat. Moving sideways, the crabs are so swift of foot they seem to glide over the sand, hardly touching it. They seem completely at home on the dry sand, and indeed they are, but they also retain a few last links with the sea.

The ghost crabs you see scuttling on the beach almost never enter the sea on purpose. About the only exceptions to this rule are if a crab is cornered and cannot get to its hole, and once yearly when the female releases her eggs.

The eggs hatch into tiny larvae, which at first mix with the billions of other minuscule floating animals and plants that make up the sea's plankton. After a while, however, the larvae begin progress toward the beach, and eventually make a landfall.

*Defiant, a young ghost crab that has been cornered away from its burrow on the sands of Assateague Island stands at bay. The creature has a body no larger than a thumbnail and is as gray as the sand.*

Ashore, the larvae excavate burrows in the sand, close to the water's edge. There they stay until they develop into perfect miniatures of the adults. It is possible to see ghost crabs that have the full adult form but are only as large as a man's thumbnail.

Early in the life of a ghost crab, it digs its hole close to the water. These holes are small, and not as obvious as those higher on the beach, which are the work of full-grown crabs. The burrows can be a yard deep. The little mounds of sand in front of them have been carted up from under the ground by the crab, whose feet make the tracks around the mouth of the hole.

While generally shunning the sea, the ghost crab needs to periodically soak itself in the wave wash. At least a couple of times each day, the crab creeps to a place where the water will surge over it, but hopefully not carry it off the beach. The reason for these occasional wettings is that the crab cannot breathe air, and must get its oxygen from the water. All it takes for the crab to do this is to moisten its gills. As long as the gills are wet the crab is free to wander far up on the beach.

The holes of the ghost crabs mark the limits of the upper beach zone. The region beyond is out of the normal reach of the sea, although by no means its impact. Even many yards inland, the only organisms which can survive are those which have adapted to the proximity of the sea. Plants, for example, must be able to tolerate wind and airborne salt spray, as well as poor soil.

*The tracks of a ghost crab and the spoils dug out of its burrow mark a beach near Cocoa Beach, Florida. From the Middle Atlantic south, beaches are riddled with such burrows but they often escape notice.*

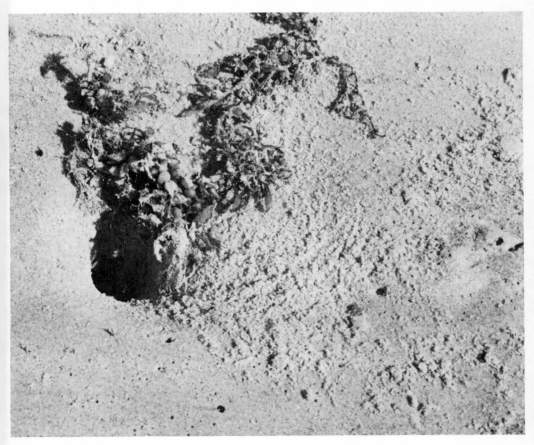

Where there is enough soil for the growth of substantial vegetation, the strong sense of zonation that characterizes the beach proper also reaches far above it. Such is the case where soil has collected in pockets between boulders overlooking rocky beaches, and especially in extensive sand dunes, where there is a definite series of zones.

Typically, the pattern of zonation begins with beach grass, or other plants which are unquestionably seaside varieties. A short distance farther back, types which are more like those growing inland begin to increase. Next, at least where people have not interfered, comes low forest, often within a few hundred yards of the beach.

Along the rocky shores of northern New England, a full-fledged forest of spruce and other conifers sometimes grows down to within a stone's throw of the black zone. The abruptness of the transition between forest and sea results from the flooding of the coastal valleys after the retreat of the last glacier.

In most places, however, the progression of vegetational zones is much more gradual. Although some species of plants may differ with geography, the general succession of the belts behind the beach is much the same everywhere.

## ABOVE THE BEACH

Only a few really pioneering plants can thrive on the face of the dunes flanking the beach, or the rocks near the black zone. Salt spray, together with the wind, make this region exceedingly inhospitable as far as plants are concerned.

Almost as primitive as the algae of the black zone are the lichens that encrust the rocks immediately above it. Lichens are not only seaside plants but grow in a variety of places from the equator to polar regions. They are the crusty mats of gray and green often found on stone walls and tree trunks.

Lichens are unusual in that they are a combination of two types of plants. Each lichen is composed of a fungus and an alga, working together for one another's benefit, a relationship called "symbiosis." The alga, as a green plant, has chlorophyll, necessary for making food through photosynthesis. The fungus, which cannot produce its own food, shares in the bounty. In return it stores water in its threads, which also secrete acids that dissolve minerals from the rock. The minerals are incorporated into the food-making process by the alga.

The threads of the fungus usually are the easiest part of a lichen to see, although some of them are so small it takes a look through a hand lens to define them. The alga is enmeshed in the mat formed by the fungus threads.

Cracks in seaside rocks harbor other unusual plants. Among these are the saltworts (*Salicornia*), also typical of salt marshes. Like desert plants, those which inhabit the margins of the sea must cope with an environment deficient in fresh water. The saltwort handles the problem much like a cactus, by storing water in its succulent tissue.

The leafless green stems of saltwort are clublike in appearance, with many branches. In the autumn, the plants blossom with myriad flowers so tiny they are difficult to discern as individuals. However, they tinge the entire plant with color, such as orange or red.

Saltwort seeds sprout when soaked by a fresh rain. The seedlings must shoot down roots quickly, before the tide next can reach them and sweep them away, often a matter of a day or two.

Not uncommonly during the late summer and autumn, the beach stroller can see the gleam of gold coming from the deep, dark crevices and hollows between the boulders of the rocky coast. Such places collect just enough soil for the growth of the seaside goldenrod (*Solidago sempervirens*). Occasionally, globs of foam wafted by the wind also catch in the niches where the goldenrod has flowered. The white mounds of foam and gold of the flowers create a singular touch of beauty among the shadows.

Seaside goldenrod also grows on the ocean face of the first, or "primary," dune line. As an adaptation to the aridity, heat, and salt, the goldenrod leaves are fleshy, thick, and tough-skinned. They grow directly off the stem.

Clinging with the goldenrod to the primary dunes are sea rocket (*Cakile eventula*) and sandbur (*Cenchrus tribuloides*). These plants are scattered among the true pioneer plant of the sandy beach, which as has been noted is American beach grass. The superb adaptation of beach grass to the dunes is shown by what happens when sand piles up around its base. To avoid being buried, the stems merely shoot higher, keeping the leaves of the plant well above the surface. This way the grass survives a condition that would kill most other plants.

When, for whatever reason, beach grass does die, however, a readily identifiable mark is left on the dune. It is a U-shaped depression, known as a "blow out," caused by the wind sweeping the sand away from a site once occupied by a clump of beach grass. The formation of a blow out is the first stage in the cycle that can lead to the destruction of the dune, and perhaps of the whole beach.

Healthy beach grass reproduces rapidly, spreading in two ways. One is by seeds from feathery white flowers. Look for them at sum-

*Seaside goldenrod is a plant with delicate flowers. Found from New Jersey north, it may reach a yard high but beaten by the sea wind, it usually is shorter.*

mer's end. Far more productive, although slower, is the other method. Along the rhizomes which stretch out under ground from each grass clump, small buds sprout, and then grow upward. When the buds burst through the surface they become tiny plants. The new plants quickly send up leaves and down roots, and eventually rhizomes spread out from them. Before long the young plants have added substantially to the underground matrix which holds the dunes in place.

Frequently, a clump of beach grass will have circular lines in the sand around it. The lines are drawn by the tips of broken stems that bend, touch the sand, and are pushed by the wind.

Beach grass really comes into its own over the crest of the primary dunes. In the sheltered troughs between the dunes it grows thickly, forming gentle meadows. The meadows are filled with many other plants, too, some of which also grow on rocky coasts if they find appropriate niches.

## THE INTERDUNE ZONE

The vegetation of the interdune zone increases with distance from the beach. The beach grass mixes with a bevy of other plants, each struggling for a foothold. Mats of a mossy plant known as beach heather (*Hudsonia tomentosa*) carpet much of the ground. Beach heather, also known as poverty grass, was put to good use by settlers who populated the coast in colonial days. They tied the clumps together for use as brooms.

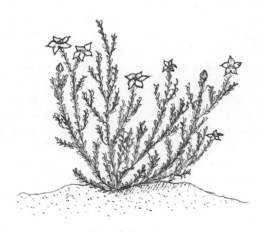

*Beach heather.*

A less desirable plant that flourishes in this zone is poison ivy (*Rhus radicans*). Where it has even the minimum of shelter, it grows thickly over the ground, and presents a hazard for the unwary. With it often grows a harmless lookalike, Virginia creeper (*Parthenocissus quinquefolia*). It is a vine with similar leaves, but they are in groups of five, rather than three, as in the ivy. Poison ivy, while distasteful for people, is a valuable wildlife food, so its presence is useful, if somewhat of a nuisance.

Notable among the plants of the interdune zone is one that many people are surprised to find along the East coast into New England. It is a cactus, the prickly pear (*Opuntia humifusa*), which forms dense mats, about a half foot or more high. Its lobes, or "joints," are flat and thick, and bear a minimum of spines, although those which are present are definitely needle sharp.

The prickly pear is a member of a group of cacti widespread in the Americas. They include the shrublike cholla of the southwestern United States, and the "tuna" of Mexico, which is the size of a small tree.

During early summer, the prickly pear brightens the beach with its yellow flowers, which are followed by small fruits, obviously pear-shaped. They are edible, and, in fact, quite tasty.

Another interdune plant with a delicious fruit is the beach plum (*Prunus maritima*), native from the Middle Atlantic states north. It can be the tallest of interdune plants, growing man high, but mostly is a low shrub. The plant can be identified by its multitude of stems and oval leaves, edged with fine teeth. The beach plum blooms in the spring, with thick clusters of white flowers. Those that flower earliest do so before even the leaves appear, making the plant readily identifiable at this time of year.

Related to the true plums, cherries, and apricots, the beach plum produces luscious fruits. The wild plant is harvested by many people, particularly for making jam. However, it is especially vulnerable to insect pests, chiefly a weevil that attacks flowers and fruit, and leaf miners, so resistant varieties of beach plum have been developed in cultivation.

Within the same geographical and environmental range as the beach plum grows the beach pea (*Lathyrus japonicus*). Like the garden variety, the beach pea has long, trailing vines, and is vivid green before ripening. Typical of so many plants adapted to the heat and dryness of the beach, the pea has leaves that are thick and leathery. Each leaf is divided into from two to a half dozen pairs of leaflets, up to two inches long. During the late spring and summer, the beach pea produces purple flowers, up to an inch long, in thick clusters.

*The hips of the rugosa rose are a remembrance of the summer, when the chill winter winds sweep the northern beaches. In summer this plant will speckle the interdune zone with flowers of red or white.*

Along the coast of central and southern Florida grows a small tree with leathery evergreen leaves, shaped like saucers, about a half foot in diameter. The tree bears fruit that resemble grapes, growing in long clusters. Not surprisingly, it is known as the sea grape. This plant is common on many Caribbean islands, often down to the upper edge of the beach.

Summer brings forth many exquisite flowers in the interdune zone. Along the northern half of the coast grows the rugosa rose (*Rosa rugosa*), a variety from China that escaped cultivation in Cape Cod more than a century ago. Three inches across, the flowers are red or white. The plant that bears them is a shrub of moderate size, up to four feet high, and growing in clumps that can be more than a dozen feet across. In autumn, after the petals drop, the fruit, or "hips," remain. They are round, the size of large olives, and shiny orange-red. Even in winter, they add a touch of color to the dunes.

Another Asian plant introduced and growing on these shores from the middle Atlantic north is the dusty miller, or beach wormwood (*Artemisia stelleriana*), which produces bright yellow blooms in mid-summer. The plant has branched, flat leaves, covered with woolly hairs, which provide insulation and also give it the "dusty" look responsible for its name. It can grow almost a yard high.

Low-lying portions of beach-grass meadows all along the coast are graced in the spring by the flowers of the sea pink (*Sabatia stellaris*). The flower is delicate, with pink petals around a yellow center that is outlined in red. Where the habitat is right, the flowers bloom profusely among the waving grass. The pink needs dampness, unlike most of the other plants described here; thus its preference for low spots. It also inhabits salt marshes.

Sharing the low places behind the primary dunes with the pink is the little seaside spurge (*Euphorbia polygonifolia*). It usually is seen only by people who look for it. Less than a foot long, the spurge hugs the sand. Its leaves are oblong and fleshy, arising from stems which turn red in the autumn.

The common dodder (*Cuscuta gronovii*) is a parasitic plant that grows among the grass and other plants of the meadows. It is a tough, twisting vine, with orange or yellow stems, that embraces its host with multiple coils. Rootless, the dodder saps its nourishment from the plants it attacks. Relatives of this plant, whose leaves are so small they resemble scales, cause great damage in clover and alfalfa fields.

Toward the inner margin of the interdune zone, the beach grass mixes with another type which at a glance resembles it. This is panic grass (*Panicum amarulum*), which grows in tufts, more thinly than beach grass. The other tall, waving plants of the dunes, in addition to the grasses, are rushes (*Juncus*) and sedges (*Scripus*). To tell the difference between the various types, examine the stems. Sedges have stems that are triangular in shape. The stems of both rushes and grasses are rounded. However, where the leaves are attached to the grass stem, the stem swells, or at least increases in thickness from the parts above and below it. The rush does not. Where sedges and rushes grow thickly in the interdune zone, a salt marsh is nearby, for these are basically wetlands plants that have invaded the sand.

Seabeach sandwort (*Arenaria peploides*) is a low plant, growing in masses from which arise myriad stems bearing fleshy, prickly leaves. Its presence signals the approaching limits of the interdune zone, because it needs a fair measure of organic soil, rather than pure sand. Intertwined among the tangle of fresh, green stems and leaves are old ones, withered and yellowing. Together, new and old vegetation make a thick carpet.

## A WALK THROUGH TIME

On wide barrier islands and along the mainland, the interdune zone gives way to scrub, and then to forest, its seaward edge stunted by wind. When the stages from beach to forest are clearly defined, undisturbed by human activity, they combine into a particularly vivid example of what scientists call "succession." That is the orderly replacement of one community of plants by another.

As a rule, under natural conditions, succession progresses from a stage in which the environment is too harsh for all but a few pioneering plants, like beach grass, to one that promotes an abundance of growth. The progression from one stage to another in a particular place usually takes many, many years, even centuries. By walking inland from the primary dunes to the forest, however, one is in effect moving through successional time. It is easy to observe how plant communities of increasing richness follow in one another's wake.

The interdune area, for example, is in an early stage of succession. The scrub behind it is a later stage, growing in soil enriched and built up by the remains of the interdune community that grew there previously. The forest is the climax of the whole process. It is safe to say that forests growing behind sand dunes stand on a site that began as beach—and probably will be again, due to the continual change at the seashore. Succession is by no means irreversible.

Of course, there are many places on the Atlantic coast where conditions differ sharply from those just described. In northern New England, only a thin line of scrub may separate the rocky shore from a wall of spruces (*Pica*), not a maritime forest but an extension of the one growing farther inland. On narrow barrier islands, the interdune corridor can be only a strip that backs up against a marsh or bay.

Not uncommonly the beach is separated vertically from the scrub by high, eroded cliffs. This is the case on some of the Georgia sea islands. In such places the scrub, and often the forest behind it, are being returned to the ocean as the bluffs are eaten away by erosion.

Undermined, the shrubs and trees crowning the bluffs fall to the beach, and remain there—skeletal forms bleached by waves and sun.

The faces of the bluffs often are flecked with the shells of oysters, clams, and similar mollusks. Some were deposited there when the site of the bluffs was right on the water. Others are refuse from the kitchens of American Indians, who long ago camped there to harvest the shellfish.

## THE SCRUB-FOREST ZONE

From Maine to Florida, one plant above all marks the beginning of the scrub-forest zone. It is the bayberry (*Myrica*). The plant is famed for its sweet-smelling berries. Boiled, they produce a wax which is used to make aromatic candles. Actually, there are two types of bayberry on our coast. The northern (*M. pensylvanica*) is a shrub that grows as far south as North Carolina. The southern (*M. cerifera*) has a northern limit of New Jersey.

It is easy to tell the difference between the two bayberries. The northern form is usually no more than waist high. The southern bayberry is a tree, forty feet tall and more than a half foot in diameter. The leaves, which are evergreen, also differ. Those on the northern bayberry are covered with gray hair. The leaves of its southern relative have a yellow tinge and spots. Furthermore, the berries of the northern plant are gray-white, while those of the southern species are light green. Only the female plants have berries.

Beach plum, poverty grass, and many other plants continue into the scrub from the interdune zone, just as a few bayberries edge into the dunes. Low junipers (*Juniperus*) grow there, too, along with wild blackberry (*Rubus*). Broom crowberry (*Corema conradii*), a spreading shrub with branches like a candelabra and needlelike evergreen leaves, adds to the thicket.

Along the southeastern coast, especially in Florida, the scrub is composed largely of saw palmetto (*Serenoa repens*). Each of its leaves is multibladed. The overall shape is one of a fan, with each blade resembling a green bayonet. Indeed, the blades are sharp, for they are studded with curved spines. Saw palmetto invades the interdune zone in some places. Where dunes are not extensive, it grows right down to the upper beach.

The farther back into the scrub one walks, the larger the trees encountered, until they form what is called maritime forest. Wading

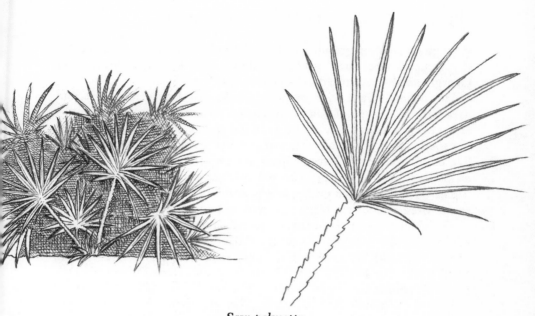

*Saw palmetto.*

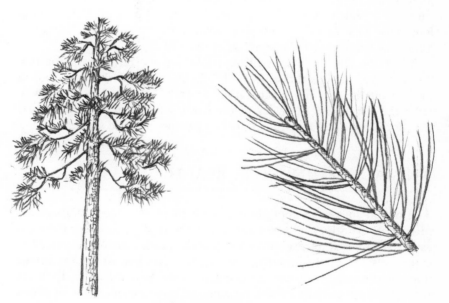

*Shortleaf pine.*

through a tangle of greenbrier (*Smilax rotundiflora*), you will eventually come to trees such as black willow (*Salix nigra*)—at least, from Georgia north—and mixed oaks (*Quercus*).

The willow, often with multiple trunks, has lanceolate leaves and dark bark. The type of oaks seen depend on geography. In the southern states the oaks likely to be growing in the scrub-forest zone are the southern red (*Q. falcata*), and the live oak (*Q. virginiana*). The live oak has elliptical leaves, which are evergreen. Its crown is especially large and spreading. The red oak has many-lobed leaves more typical of the oaks as a group, and is deciduous. Northern oaks of the scrub forest include the black (*Q. velutina*) and white (*Q. alba*).

The chief trees of the maritime forest, however, are the pines. Several types grow near beaches on the Atlantic coast. The shortleaf pine (*Pinus echinata*) has an extensive range, from Georgia to Long Island, New York. The loblolly pine (*P. taeda*) grows from Delaware's Delmarva Peninsula to central Florida. The scrub pine (*P. virginiana*) is found on the middle Atlantic coast. The pitch pine (*P. rigida*) ranges from the middle Atlantic to Maine, and is the typical shore pine of New England.

A good way of identifying pines is by their needles. Shortleaf needles are three to five inches long and come in bunches of two. The loblolly has needles six to nine inches long, yellow-green in color, and three to a bunch. Virginia pine needles are an inch to three inches long, two to a bundle. Pitch-pine needles are three to five inches in length, and similar in color to those of the loblolly.

All of the trees of the maritime forest are severely weatherbeaten. None grow as tall as the same kinds inland. Many of the trees looked pruned on the top and often rather severely in one direction, away from the sea. This is the work of the wind, which can cause trees near the shore, especially in exposed sites, to assume fantastic shapes.

## ANIMALS BEHIND THE BEACH

The region above the upper beach is inhabited by a surprising variety of animals. Mostly, they are creatures of the land, or at least of the air, rather than the water, so are not confined to any particular zone. Except for some of the seabirds, the animals that live or forage in the dunes and scrub forest are not peculiar to the beach. Rather, they are the same types as those inhabiting adjacent areas inland. Some of them, moreover, actually live away from the shore but visit there to take advantage of the sea's bounty.

# TIGER BEETLES

Of the host of creeping, crawling, and flying insects swarming in the area behind the beach, the tiger beetle is among the most interesting. Tiger beetles (*Cicindelidae*) are astoundingly swift, active hunters which thrive on sand and sunshine, so the dunes are a perfect home for them. Hot, sunny days send them into a frenzy of activity.

Equipped with sickle-shaped mandibles, which cross when at rest and can even give humans a painful bite, the tiger beetles are the terror of smaller insects. About a half inch long, tiger beetles come in a variety of colors, from metallic blue, orange, or bronze, to a pale color matching the sand. Some have brilliant patterns on their backs.

Typically, a tiger beetle waits quietly in ambush for other insects to pass by. When something suitable comes close enough, the beetle rushes out, and grabs the victim in its powerful, pincerlike jaws.

Even in the larval stage, as a grub, the tiger beetle is a savage predator. The grub resembles a humpbacked worm with a large head and powerful jaws. After hatching from an egg laid in the sand, the grub spends its time in an inch-deep burrow. Hooks on the grub's body anchor it in place, with its head poking out the burrow door. The head and neck effectively plug up the door so that other insects do not detect it. Some come so close they even tread upon the grub's head, a fatal mistake.

Once the prey is within range the grub grabs it with the curved jaws that are the beetle's trademark even before reaching adult form. The victim is hauled into the burrow and eaten, or if still alive beaten senseless against the walls of the hole, then devoured.

Once matured, a tiger beetle is capable of flight, and, in fact, quite good at it. If you happen to startle a tiger beetle, the chances are it will buzz into the air, fly several yards, and then alight, keeping a look out for the source of the disturbance.

# WOLF SPIDERS

Burrowing wolf spiders (*Geolycosa*) are also hunters of great skill. Built for speed, they have long, powerful legs on which they race after prey. They do most of their hunting by night, rather than in daylight like the tiger beetle. After dawn, the wolf spider is likely to be found in its burrow, which may reach a yard deep into the sand. When excavating its home, the spider ties together loose sand grains with silk, and tosses them to the surface. Sometimes the sand forms small rings around the mouth of the burrow.

Rather hairy, the wolf spider matches the color of the sand. It looks ferocious, and from the standpoint of the insects it preys upon certainly is, but it is not at all a threat to people.

# FROGS AND TOADS

Although amphibians such as frogs and toads cannot survive in salt water, several live in the interdune and scrub-forest zones. This is especially true if pockets exist where fresh water can collect, or where small freshwater marshes have formed in the maritime forest. Amphibians need moisture as adults, although they breathe air, and they lay their eggs in the water, where the larvae go through a gilled tadpole stage.

One toad is especially at home in sandy places and thus common in the two zones. Fowler's toad (*Bufo woodhousei*) ranges from New England into North Carolina along the coast, and farther south inland. It is typical of the animals one thinks of as toads—warty, brown or rust-colored, squat, and bulging of eye. Like most other amphibians, the toad is active mostly at night, especially during warm rains. It gathers in small bodies of water, even flooded ditches, to breed from late spring to early autumn. When breeding, the males call for their mates with a sound that resembles a short, flat bleat.

Like the Fowler's toad, the southern toad (*Bufo terrestris*) is partial to sandy places, and can be found behind the beach from Virginia to Florida. The two toads look very much alike, but there are a few ways in which you can tell them apart without being an expert on amphibians. Most toads have a series of ridges and knobs atop their heads, but the southern toad also has a pair of very large bumps, set back between the eyes. No other toad in its region has them. Also, check the number of warts in each spot on the toad. If there are just one or two warts per spot, the chances are—although not every single time—that it is the southern species.

Unlike the Fowler's toad, the southern type has a very musical call, a high-pitched trill that can last for more than six seconds. The southern toad calls during rainy periods between spring and midautumn.

From the Delmarva Peninsula all the way down through the Florida Keys lives the green tree frog (*Hyla cinerea*), whose clangorous breeding calls can be heard any time from early spring to late autumn. This frog, two inches long and greenish-yellow, sounds like the clang of a brassy bell. Its call is loud, and delivered rapid fire. Often hundreds of frogs will be calling at once from a small pool in the maritime forest or even in the brush of the dunes, producing enough noise to wake up anyone who happens to be sleeping nearby.

Like other tree frogs, the green species has toes tipped with adhesive disks, permitting it to climb with ease, even on vertical surfaces. Green tree frogs venture deep into the dunes, right down to the edge of the beach. They sometimes climb the walls of beach cottages and outbuildings, as they search for insects to eat. Outdoor beach showers seem to be a favorite retreat of this frog, most likely because of the fresh water and humidity the animal finds in them. The frogs also turn up outside the lighted windows of cottages during the night to feast on the insects which the illumination has drawn there.

The leopard frog (*Rana pipiens*) is likely to be found near the beach anywhere along the coast, and in some places is quite common in the scrub or maritime forest. This species is brown, sometimes with a green shade, and is covered on its back and sides with large dark spots, which are rounded in shape. The southern race of leopard frog, particularly, is a seaside inhabitant, and even ventures into brackish water, an unusual place to find an amphibian.

## SNAKES

Where there are toads, almost certainly the hognose snake (*Heterodon*) lives, too, as is the case behind the dunes along all the coast south of Maine. The hognose snake, an inveterate eater of toads is not very large, often less than two feet long, although it occasionally reaches a yard. Known for its consummate acting ability, the serpent has two distinct and impressive routines with which it attempts to dissuade an enemy from harming it.

When alarmed, the hognose snake first tries bluff. Flattening its head and neck, the snake rears back, puffs up with air, and hisses menacingly. The act can be quite convincing to people who are not able to identify a hognose, for the creature looks every bit as dangerous as a cottonmouth or rattlesnake. If its enemy does not back down, however, the hognose reveals its true nature, and flops over, belly up, as if dead. It even jerks about a few times, as if in the last throes of life, before "expiring," with its tongue hanging out of its mouth. The bluff fails, however, because the hognose goes overboard with its act. Turned on its belly, the supposedly dead snake will quickly flop over on its back once more.

The best way to identify a hognose is by its distinctly upturned

snout. No other snake has such a snub nose. Its color is highly varia-
ble, from yellow to brown, but it almost always is spotted. Its stomach is lighter in color than its back.

Hognose snakes are normally considered harmless, and for all prac-
tical purposes, they are. However, the hognose is one of the increasing
number of allegedly harmless serpents which in the last few years have
been implicated in venomous bites. At least two cases have been re-
ported in which people were bitten by hognose snakes and suffered
some pain and swelling in the region of the bite.

Like the hognose, the common water snakes (*Natrix*) often are
mistaken for highly dangerous serpents. This is particularly true of the
brown water snake (*N. taxispilota*), which ranges from Virginia
south, and the northern water snake (*N. sipedon*) living from North
Carolina to Maine. They have a very close resemblance to the highly
venomous cottonmouth (*Agkistrodon piscivorus*), which from Virginia south frequents the same habitats. All three snakes thrive in
swamps, marshes, pools, and rivers. Where there is fresh water close to
the seashore, these snakes can be found there.

All are dark-colored and good-sized, easily a yard in length and
quite thick. The back of water snakes and younger cottonmouths are
marked with bands and blotches, but these often are obscured by the
body color or by mud. Underneath, the water snakes have spots and
other markings that are much more evident. Within the range of the
cottonmouth, however, it does not pay to go too close to any large,
dark snake found in wet places. If the snake happens to be a cottonmouth, and is aroused, it will open its jaws wide and reveal the trait
responsible for its name—the snow-white lining of its mouth.

The coast from North Carolina to Key West is also the home of another serpent that is very dangerous, the eastern diamondback rattlesnake (*Crotalus adamanteus*). This big snake, which can reach eight
feet in length, prefers dry, sandy habitats, such as among beach pines
and palmettos. It is not shy of salt water, and, in fact, even voyages
out into the ocean, to make a landfall on small islands.

On the back of the serpent are the markings that distinguish it, dark
diamonds outlined in yellow, or sometimes cream. There is no mistak-
ing this snake, which remains common where human settlement is not
dense.

Fortunately, the diamondback will begin to rattle when a person is
at a considerable distance, even several yards away. If pressed, the
snake will usually attempt to escape, although it will strike if cornered.

The likelihood of being bitten by a diamondback or any other venomous snake along southern beaches is extremely slight, even though the serpents exist there. The snakes, despite their fangs and venom, are retiring animals, not aggressive unless pushed. Statistically, moreover, there is less chance in the United States of a person dying from snakebite than from the sting of a bee. At the same time, if one is walking in country where such serpents are known to live, it is a good idea to exercise a bit of caution about where one places one's hands and feet, and sits down.

The eastern garter snake (*Thamnophis sirtalis*), which exists along all of the coast, frequently is seen in the scrub-forest and interdune zones. It is a slender snake, about two feet long, with three longitudinal stripes, usually yellow, against its dark back. Although a species of western garter snake has been cited among the so-called harmless serpents that under some circumstances can be mildly venomous, the eastern type offers no real threat to people.

## LIZARDS

Especially along the southern half of the coast, several lizards may be seen near the beach. Prominent among these reptiles are the sand skink (*Neoseps reynoldsi*) which roams the back dunes in Florida, and the six-lined racerunner (*Cnemidophorus sexlineatus*), ranging from Maryland south.

The skink is a finger-length creature which has legs so small they are easy to overlook. This is particularly true of the front pair, which are practically enclosed by a fold in the side of the body.

Actually, the limbs are of little importance to the skink, which burrows like a worm through the sand. Even its snout, shaped like a wedge, is an adaptation for pushing through the sand in which the lizard lives. The limbless appearance of the skink is its most distinguishing characteristic. The color is bland, from light yellow to brown.

Contrasting with the skink, the racerunner has long, powerful legs that speed this half-foot lizard over the ground with dazzling swiftness. Pale brown, with a long, thin tail, the racerunner is so fast it can afford to spend much of its time in the open. If alarmed, it dashes to the nearest hiding place and promptly vanishes. The racerunner likes sandy places, so it comes quite close to the beach in its wanderings. If you happen to get close enough, you may see the six light stripes that identify it.

# BIRDS BEHIND THE DUNES

Most of the birds that can be seen in neighboring inland areas also frequent the life zones behind the beach. So do many birds of the immediate waterfront. Certain birds, however, are more than casual visitors, and find the habitats near the shore so inviting they are very common there. Others use the inland fringes of the beach for specific activities, such as nesting, so are likely to be seen there at the appropriate times.

Among the latter are the terns. Various species of terns breed in the interdune zone, as long as the environment is not disturbed. The most abundant species, ranging along the entire coast, is the common tern (*Sterna hirundo*). A sleek bird, smaller than a gull, with the pointed wings that distinguish the terns, it is light gray above and snow white underneath. It has a tail that is sharply forked and a black cap.

Similar in appearance to its common cousin is the roseate tern (*Sterna dougallii*), seen in summer on the northern half of the coast. Distinguishing one species from the other is difficult. The tail of the roseate tern, however, is longer, and in the breeding season the bill of the common type undergoes a change in color. Normally, the bill of both terns is dark. During the spring and early summer, when the terns are reproducing, the portion of the common tern's bill behind the tip turns orange, so vivid it sometimes can be seen while the bird is flying overhead.

Both terns nest in hollows in the sand. The common tern sometimes rears its young right on the beach, but usually selects a place just within the seaward fringes of the beach grass. The roseate tern likes more cover, and tends to nest deeper in the beach grass meadows.

If you should happen to disturb a tern's nest—something that should be avoided—the young will scurry into the nearest grass thicket. Splotched with brown, they easily blend into the sand and vegetation. The parents, meanwhile, circle overhead, screaming loudly. Sometimes they swoop down, as if to attack. This behavior, however, is not an assault, but rather an attempt to distract the interloper so the young can dash off unseen. If you pay no attention to the adults, but keep an eye peeled on the ground nearby, you may be rewarded by seeing two or three little balls of fluff on stick legs skittering for a hiding place.

Scrub-forest and coastal conifer groves almost anywhere on the Atlantic shore are likely to be the year-round home of chickadees (*Parus*), and rest areas for migrating wood warblers (Parulidae). Large numbers of warblers—small, colorful, and active—find temporary haven in coastal woodlands as they travel between southern wintering grounds and northern breeding areas. Warbler migrations are at their height in May, and between mid-August and late September.

The warblers usually travel at night, stopping with the dawn. Once a flight has landed the little birds hop and flit among the trees for hours at a time, making the woods buzz with their activity. There are dozens of species, many quite similar in appearance, and difficult to identify for all but expert birders. What is more, warblers tend to travel in mixed flocks, aggravating the problem of identification. Even if the species in a flight cannot be distinguished, however, watching the bright, perky birds is a distinct pleasure.

The seasons of migration increase the numbers of birds of prey that patrol the environs of the beach. Red-tailed hawks (*Buteo jamaicensis*) live year round all along the coast, but tend to congregate in southern areas during the winter. These are large hawks, with a four-foot wingspan. They are identified by the rusty color on the top surface of their tail feathers.

Commonest small hawk of the interdune area is the sparrow hawk (*Falco sparverius*), a tiny falcon that likes open and lightly wooded country. It often is seen perching on telephone wires, or hovering in one place while on the wing. Mainly an insect eater, it has a rusty back and light chest, with bluish wings.

When extremely severe winter weather sweeps northern Canada, one of the most spectacular of all North American birds frequently seeks refuge along the coast as far south as North Carolina. It is the snowy owl (*Nyctea scandaiaca*), a fierce hunter of the tundra. Young birds, particularly, show up on occasion along our shores, not right on the water but very close to it. The younger owls are touched with brown, and are thus darker than the full-grown adults.

The sighting of snowy owls in winter is not as uncommon as might be believed, especially north of New York. Almost every winter, a few of these spectacular birds, which have a wingspan of almost five feet, are seen in the sand dunes, or sometimes the marshes, of places such as Cape Cod, and coastal Connecticut.

## MAMMALS

As is the case with birds, mammals found near the beach are the same types as live farther inland. Because they are much more secretive and mainly nocturnal, however, the mammals seldom are seen by beach-walkers. Hidden from view are myriad small creatures such as the

*Snowy owl.*

white-footed mouse (*Peromyscus leucopus*) and the least shrew (*Cryptotis parva*). More easily seen—and, indeed, probably the wild mammal spotted most near our beaches—is the cottontail rabbit (*Sylvilagus floridanus*). Occasionally, around dawn or dusk, a raccoon (*Procyon lotor*) can be spied on its way to forage at the strand line. So can the striped skunk (*Mephitis mephitis*). These two animals remain active most of the winter. Their tracks are much more easily seen in the snow than in the sand.

Walkers in the lands abutting the seashore should keep an eye peeled for another mammal that sometimes can be glimpsed before sunset or around dawn. The white-tailed deer (*Odocoileus virginianus*) fares very well in seashore habitats, and requires only a bit of cover, not real wilderness, to prosper. Where extensive grass meadows lie in the interdune zone, the deer will come out to feed. They also come close to the sea in search of the lush grasses that grow in salt marshes.

# 6

# *Backwaters—*
# *Marshes and Mangroves*

Where the seashore has been left in a relatively natural state, the scrub and stunted forest behind the dunes often back up in turn upon salt marsh or, in southern Florida, its ecological counterpart, the mangrove swamp. These two habitats form only where the power of the waves is sufficiently decreased for particulate matter to settle and build up into shoals, the first step in their creation.

As a rule, such protection is found in the backwaters of embayments and estuaries, which also serve as settling basins for particles, drained from the land as well as swept in from the sea. Under the right conditions shoals develop into mudflats, which are readily colonized by salt-marsh cordgrass or red mangrove, as the case may be. These salt-resistant plants anchor the mud in place, and the flats grow into small islands. Eventually, the level of the mud is raised enough for the establishment of new plants less tolerant of the daily submergence in salt water that is withstood by the cordgrass and red mangrove.

Marshes and mangrove habitats vary immensely in extent. The marshes behind the barrier islands of South Carolina and Georgia, for example, stretch for several miles before reaching the mainland. Among the rocks of New England, on the other hand, a full-fledged salt marsh may grow within the arms of a rocky cove with a diameter measured only in yards.

The whole tip of the Florida peninsula is fringed by a vast mangrove swamp, shielded by the keys and grading imperceptibly from the land into the sea. A hundred miles or so to the north, the mangroves show up mostly as narrow strips of green edging the banks of coastal rivers and inlets.

*Mallard ducks preen while the tide is out at a salt marsh in eastern Connecticut. At low water the rich layers of marsh soil are visible. This scene is along a tidal creek, which flushes the marsh, mixing nutrients of sea and land.*

## THE IMPORTANCE OF MARSHES AND MANGROVES

Where they grow profusely, marshes and mangroves guard the mainland behind them against severe storm damage by absorbing the energy of powerful storm waves. Above all, however, it is the richness of these habitats that makes them important, far beyond their boundaries. Of the two, the marsh is most productive along our coast, both relatively and totally.

In terms of productivity, the salt marsh generates more organic matter than a healthy grainfield. Some parts of our marshes annually produce more than ten tons of nutrients per acre, more than half of which is not needed by the marsh and swept away to enrich the sea.

The decay of the vegetation grown by the marsh may smell bad but it is a sign of a healthy life cycle. Some of the vegetation decays in the form of detritis, mentioned in an earlier chapter. At the same time, the marsh mud teems with decomposers such as bacteria. Although they are microscopic, bacteria in salt marshes sometimes occur in colonies large enough so that their traces are visible to the unaided eye. You have found one if you come upon a spot where the mud has a distinct purple tinge. The color results from a colony of purple sulphur bacteria under the surface of the mud.

The bacteria are anaerobic, that is, they do not function in the presence of oxygen. If a thick blanket of silt and other particles cover the mud, air does not penetrate and anaerobic conditions occur, encouraging the growth of the purple sulphur bacteria. They steadily decompose cordgrass and other organic materials, enriching both marsh and sea. The anaerobic decay of vegetation in a healthy marsh produces a slight odor, like that of rotten eggs. As long as the smell is not overpowering, it is a good sign. Too potent an odor, however, means the marsh is not faring well, generally because the flow of the tide has been blocked from renewing the oxygen in its creeks and pools.

Incoming tides bring fresh water and oxygen to the marsh, roiling the nutrients so that when the tide changes they will be carried out to sea. The alternate filling and flushing of the marsh keeps it vital; conversely, draining a salt marsh or blocking it from the sea causes its death.

Mangroves, like the marshes, produce immense quantities of rich detritus. The main source of the detritus is the mangrove leaf. When it falls into the water it quickly is coated with bacteria and fungi, which begin to decompose it. Attracted by the prospect of eating the decomposers, other microscopic organisms swarm to the leaf, further covering it. The leaf is broken down to small bits—detritus—still covered with tiny organisms. Together, the fragment of leaf and its passengers make a nourishing tidbit for all sorts of marine animals, from shrimp to fish.

Vast amounts of nutrients, mixing in a veritable soup, make the sheltered waters of the marsh and mangroves a prime nursery area for fish. Other fish regularly visit the backwaters to feed. All told, the vast majority of commercially harvested fish and shellfish depend on these for habitats during at least one part of their life cycles.

*A "pencil" of red mangrove is sprouting in a tidal area of the Florida Keys. Mangrove swamps form an immense wilderness over much of the southern tip of the Florida peninsula and on to the Keys. People have been lost in the mangroves for days while canoeing.*

# VEGETATION OF THE MARSH

The cordgrass, which is the first major vegetation of the marsh, hugs the area which is regularly flooded by the tide. Where the tidal range is great, and the low marsh zone is wide, there is an abundant growth of cordgrass. In places where there is a small difference between high and low tide, however, the low marsh zone is narrow, and the cordgrass belt correspondingly restricted. The largest portions of such marshes usually are covered by salt-meadow hay. It grows on elevations of a few inches to a foot above the mean high-tide line, covered with water only during the spring tide. Mixed with the hay in northern marshes is the black rush (*Juncus gerardi*), and from Maryland south, black needlerush (*Juncus roemerianus*).

Black rush is short, delicate, and dark green. Needlerush is the same color, much darker than the salt-meadow hay, but stiff and thick. Atop its stem is a long leaf with a sharp point that gives needlerush its name. The two rushes grow thickly toward the highest portions of the upper marsh zone, bordering the uplands.

Salt marsh bulrush (*Scirpus robustus*), really a sedge, grows toward the rear of the marsh, and is a valuable wildlife food. Up to five feet tall, it is dark green in color.

From mudflats through the marsh zones to upland, successional patterns are just as evident as they are behind the dunes. The mudflats represent the early stages of the marsh. The cordgrass is next, followed by the hay, and then the plants that grow between the marsh proper and the uplands.

Exploring a marsh is fun, for it has a more mysterious aspect than the other seaside habitats. However, it is not easy. The muck is deep, and sometimes presents a hazard. One must be careful not to fall into one of the many creeks, some of which are hidden or appear much more shallow than they are. Perhaps the least strenuous way to have a look at a salt marsh is to explore its edges. The best way to cover as much as possible is to travel the creeks and channels by canoe or kayak. Such craft can move silently, without alarming wildlife, and because they can glide over only a few inches of water can carry you right into the heart of the marsh. Remember, however, that when the tide goes out, a flowing marsh creek can turn into a mudbank, leaving the boat and its passengers stranded until it fills again.

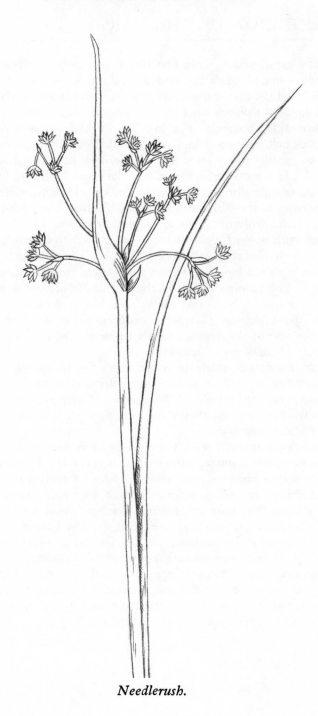

*Needlerush.*

# MORE MARSH PLANTS

Because few plants are as tolerant of salt water as the cordgrass, it shares the lower marsh zone with hardly any other species. Beginning at the mean high-tide line and continuing through the upper marsh zone, however, an increasing number of plants appear. Many are the same that grow behind the beach, but several are especially characteristic of marshes.

One of the species growing closest to the tide line is salt grass (*Distichlis spicata*), which is able to survive flooding by sea water more than the salt-meadow hay, but less than cordgrass. It is two feet tall at highest, so it is usually shorter than the hay. Salt-grass leaves sprout from opposite sides of the stem, not all around it, as in the case of the hay. The light green clusters of salt-grass flowers bloom after those of the hay, in late summer and autumn.

From Virginia south, the upper marsh zone is the home of sea oxeye (*Borrichia frutescens*). It is a low shrub, with thick, spoon-shaped leaves, and grows in dense bunches. Its yellow flowers, standing on stems above the leaves, appear in midsummer.

During August, splashes of lavender appear among the salt-meadow hay. The color is caused by tiny but massed flowers of sea lavender (*Limonium*), which grows on lacy stems, up to two feet high, above a mat of leathery green leaves. The leaves are so tough they often remain for the winter, after the stems shrivel, and until they are pushed aside by the new year's growth.

On northern shores, among the very first flowers to bloom in the marsh is silverweed (*Potentilla anserina*). The flowers of this plant, which resembles a strawberry and has leaves with silvery undersides, are yellow, and can be almost an inch in diameter. Toward the end of summer, the silverweed bears fruit that resemble little blackberries.

An indisputable sign that the upper limits of the marsh have been reached, and some fresh water is present, are the spectacular flowers of the rose mallow (*Hibiscus moscheutos*). Growing along all but the northern extremity of the coast, this plant has blooms that sometimes reach more than a half foot in diameter. Resembling the flowers of the hollyhock, only larger, they are pink, sometimes to the point of being rosy. The flowers bloom in August and September. During the rest of the growing season, the plant can be told by its olive-colored leaves, three-lobed, tapered, and the size of a man's hand. The plant is shrubby, but not even a foot high.

Found on most of the Atlantic seaboard, the marsh elder (*Iva frutescens*), or highwater shrub, marks the upland boundary of the salt marsh. Not more than twelve feet high, often much less, the elder has tapered, tooth-edged leaves three or four inches across, and sprouting opposite one another on the stem. The greenish-white flowers are small and inconspicuous.

The high ground at the edges of a salt marsh is the natural home of a tall grass with a feathery flower head, often waving in the breeze a dozen feet above the ground. The plant is the reed grass (*Phragmites communis*), which, ironically, has spread because of the dredging, filling, and pollution of our marshlands.

Reed grass normally tries to invade the marsh from higher ground by infiltrating the low-lying areas with its long, creeping rhizomes. Under natural conditions, these assaults never are more than partly successful, and the reed grass is kept at bay in its normal habitat. In some of the low, muddy places from which reed grass has been driven back, the tracks of its rhizomes can be seen long afterward in the muck, a network of straight lines, many yards long.

Once the bottom is dredged and the spoil dumped on a marsh, however, the level of the surface is raised high enough for reed grass to gain a foothold. It quickly spreads and overcomes all the other major forms of vegetation, except at its edges, where various species manage to survive. The same result occurs when a marsh is drained, or tide gates are installed to block the normal filling and flushing cycle. Reed grass, moreover, is tough, and survives in places too polluted for salt-marsh hay and most other marsh plants. Up and down the coast, vast fields of reed grass now stand where normal marshes once grew. Reed grass has become one of the most familiar plants of the seashore.

Especially when it is tossing in the wind, or when the rays of the sun slant through its feathery heads, reed grass presents an exquisite sight. All of the windblown plumes face the same direction because they can turn a full circle. Be that as it may, however, its extreme abundance is a sign that the balance of nature in the salt marsh has been upset, and the environment degraded.

Where reed grass has taken over the site of ruined marshes, it is a mixed blessing. On the negative side, it fills and clogs creeks and channels. It keeps out other plants. Wildlife finds little in the way of food from reed grass. As the grass puts out an increasing matrix of rhizomes, more and more soil gathers around it, further raising the level of the land and eliminating the marsh.

At the same time, however, reed grass performs some functions that are very useful. It may not be a prime source of food for wildlife but provides wonderful cover, especially for waterfowl, wading birds, and red-winged blackbirds. By holding the soil, reed grass prevents erosion, so that at least there is a site surviving for possible restoration of healthy marshlands in the future.

Reed grass also helps purify contaminated water. By using the nutrients in sewage, it reduces this common sort of pollution. The grass also takes up phosphates, one of the contaminants from agricultural fertilizers, and seems to break down oil slicks.

Reed grass may be a sign of environmental destruction, but it also can work in the eleventh hour to preserve what is left of a marsh in hopes that the future will reverse the damage.

The incredible adaptability of reed grass is demonstrated not only by its ability to survive in environments damaged by human activity, but also in the astonishing range of places it inhabits naturally. Of ancient lineage, reed grass was in existence long before the first ice age—this is known from fossilized specimens. The grass literally inhabits all continents, even the edge of Antarctica. As well as seaside, it grows near freshwater marshes, including those high in the mountains of central Asia.

Around the world, reed grass has provided the raw materials for all sorts of implements and shelters. The tough stems are used in the construction of a variety of dwellings: those of the so-called "marsh Arabs" of the Middle East, the blinds of duck hunters in the United States, and the domelike homes of muskrats. Reed grass symbolizes how beneficent nature can be when balanced, and how it can run wild when disturbed.

# PLANTS OF THE MANGROVES

Mangroves, like the salt marshes farther north, have felt the impact of draining and dredging, although increased environmental awareness and protective legislation has halted the worst of the destruction. So long as they are not subject to the mass assault of dredges and bulldozers, mangroves will thrive, because the pioneer of the mangrove swamp, the red species, has the ability to spread like wildfire.

The dispersal of the red mangrove is enhanced by the way its large, rusty seeds germinate, which occurs while the seeds still are on the tree. A shoot like a small pencil erupts from the one seed within each of the mangrove fruits, growing almost a foot long before detaching and dropping from the tree into the water. Sometimes a fallen sprout roots in the shallows near the parent tree. More likely, however, it will drift, sometimes for months and even across the ocean, until it finally winds up in a mudflat or sandbar on which it can root.

By the time the shoot arrives at a suitable anchorage, it is floating upright because its roots have absorbed enough water to tilt them down. Touching the bottom, the roots grab hold and the young tree quickly grows. Its green pencil pokes above the surface of the water and is easy to spot.

Within a couple of years, the new mangrove has arched out its prop roots and dropped seeds, which are producing additional trees nearby. The formation of a mangrove swamp has begun in earnest.

From that point on, the familiar successional pattern takes hold, with the black mangrove occupying the ground that has built up around the original colonizers. Eventually, as the interior of the swamp becomes virtually dry land, the white mangrove mixes with the black.

As in the salt marsh, a large variety of plants grows only toward the upper portions of the mangrove swamp. Among the only noticeable species in the red mangroves are air plants, which have no roots and instead perch high on the branches of the trees, literally drawing nourishment out of thin air. One prominent member of the group likely to be seen on the mangroves is Spanish moss (*Tillandsia us-neoides*). This beard of vegetation is not moss at all, but a member of the pineapple family (Bromeliaceae). Among the black and white mangroves can be found another air plant, the strangler fig (*Ficus aurea*), a parasite that eventually kills the tree it embraces.

The strangler begins as a vine. Slowly, it climbs up a host tree, entwining about it tightly. Ascending to a height of dozens of feet, the vine grows thicker, and eventually sends down whiplike aerial roots, which finally sink into the ground. As the fig continues to grow, it virtually covers the tree which it has parasitized, and takes on the appearance of a tree itself. The host, meanwhile, is smothered.

Sharing the upper swamp with the white mangrove is its cousin, the buttonwood (*Concarpus erectus*). Its leaves are two to four inches long, tapering to a pointed tip. The scaly bark is dark, even black on some trees. It signifies that the mangrove swamp has reached its landward limits, a statement supported by the fact that a few cabbage palms (*Sabal palmetto*), really inland trees, often can be seen growing near the buttonwoods.

Mangroves and marshes have a number of animals in common with each other and also with other habitats beyond the open beach front. White-tailed deer, raccoons, cottonmouths, and herons are as much at home in the marsh as other surroundings already mentioned. The backwater habitats, however, have some inhabitants that are truly characteristic of, and often even critical to, their existence.

*New mangrove islands are beginning in the shallow water of Florida Bay. If left alone, these little clumps will grow, their roots trap debris, and new land will form amid the spreading mangrove thickets.*

## FISH OF MARSH AND MANGROVE

An inclusive account of the fish that inhabit or visit the backwaters would read like a listing of most Atlantic coast species. Some, however, are much more likely to be seen than others, and are described here.

The various mummichogs discussed in the chapter about the life at the water's edge live in the shallows of the marsh as well as those elsewhere on the waterfront. Particularly common is the common mummichog, finger length and very heavily built for its size. It is dark green, and has stripes in the breeding season only. It ranges all along the coast. Also in the backwaters are silversides, which dart about the cordgrass jungle at high tide. During the early summer, the silversides spawn among the marsh grasses, where vast numbers of eggs are released.

Each egg is tiny, hardly more than a millimeter in diameter, but it is big enough to hold an embryonic fish, which hatches in about a week. The eggs would be virtually impossible to see if it were not for the fact that they stick together in ropy clusters attached to the bases of the grass, and the bottom. The eggs mass because each has a tail of adhesive filaments, which entangles the eggs and also weights them down so they sink toward the bottom. If you happen to encounter silversides at the moment of spawning, you may notice the water is clouded with milky color. This is the milt of the males, which fertilizes the eggs once they are released by the females.

A graphic example of the importance of the salt marsh and mangroves to the production of a valuable fish is the case of the menhaden (*Brevoortia tyrannus*), or mossbunker.

A foot long, blue-green on the top and silvery underneath, the menhaden is best identified by a dark spot just behind each gill opening. An oily fish, it is not sought for human consumption, but nevertheless is extremely important, both to sports anglers and commercial fishermen. Menhaden are a prime prey—and thus bait—for many larger species, including bluefish, striped bass, and weakfish. Moreover, menhaden are the source of fish meal for livestock, and fertilizer. As such they are the basis of one of the largest commercial fisheries on the coast.

Menhaden are warm-water fish, migrating north in the spring, retreating south in autumn. They travel in large schools, close to the surface. In bright sunlight the schools sometimes resemble dark shadows moving through the water. Menhaden penetrate far up rivers and into the salt marshes and mangroves, favorite feeding grounds, because they eat detritus.

Although menhaden spawn at sea, the young fish head into the marshes and mangroves to mature. In the North, the approach of winter chills the marsh waters and sends the young, with the adults, on their southward migration.

The mullet (*Mugil cephalus*) has a similar relationship to the salt marsh and mangrove swamp, maturing in the shallows, and later returning as an adult to feed on detritus. A sizable fish, the mullet sometimes exceeds two feet in length. Like the menhaden, it roams in large schools, which ripple the surface. Typical of many schooling fish, the mullet is dark above, light silvery on the sides and below. This pattern of coloration—also found in menhaden, tuna, and mackerel—is known as countershading, and is a form of natural camouflage.

When a countershaded fish is seen from below, its light underside blends with the illumination at the surface. From above, the dark back of the fish is easily lost in the dimness of the depths.

The onset of spring brings runs of a fish called the alewife (*Pomolobus pseudoharengus*) into the salt-marsh creeks and other rivers that empty into the sea as far south as North Carolina. Slightly more than a foot long, alewives look like chunky herring or small shad, to which they are related. Silvery and streamlined despite their heavy build, the alewives spawn upstream and then depart before the arrival of the menhaden, with which they might be confused. When alewives are running up a river, they repeatedly leap and splash on the surface; when the run is extremely heavy, the water churns with their bodies. People often snag and net them to use as bait for game fish.

Alewives spend most of their lives at sea, but hatch in freshwater streams and ponds linked to the ocean. The young head downstream for the sea when only a few weeks old. By autumn they begin life as marine fish. Alewives eat plankton and smaller fish, including their own kind.

The characteristic large schooling fish of the red mangroves is the mangrove snapper (*Lutjanus griseus*), which is gray to reddish in color and sometimes weighs more than a dozen pounds. Large schools of snappers hover in the water about the mangrove roots, where the crabs and other small creatures on which they prey abound.

Among the mangrove roots also patrol schools of brown grunts (*Haemulon parra*). Much smaller than the snapper, the grunt does not exceed a foot in length and a half pound in weight. Its body is shiny gray, with brown streaks.

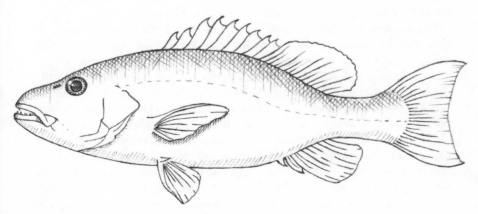

*Mangrove snapper.*

The brackish water of the black mangrove swamp is the home of certain small fish which also inhabit fresh waters inland, and are commonly kept in home aquariums. One is the sailfin mollie (*Mollienisia latipinna*), a three-inch algae eater, with an olive body and a huge dorsal fin of shiny blue. The other is the minuscule mosquito fish (*Gambusia affinis*), about two inches long, and an avid eater of mosquito larvae. Because of its diet, the mosquito fish has been introduced in warm lands around the world as a means of controlling malaria. The mosquito fish resembles the guppy, but is not as colorful. It is pale gray, although the male is splotched with dark markings.

## CRABS

The exposed tidal flats around the mangroves and the slick banks of marsh creeks are often riddled with small holes, about the diameter of a little finger. These are the burrows of fiddler crabs (*Uca*), relatives of the ghost crab but much smaller, in fact not much bigger than a nickel when adult. The fiddler gets its name from the super size of one of the two pincerlike claws on the male. The big claw is the "fiddle," the smaller one the fiddler's "bow."

If undisturbed, the fiddlers arise from their burrows at ebb tide and patrol the mud in large squadrons. An inner biological clock tells the crabs that the tide has retreated so they can forage for something to eat. The crabs feed on decaying pieces of cordgrass, mangrove leaves, and other detritus. They scoop up detritus-laden mud in their claws, and sort out the food in their mouths, ejecting the mud. This process, plus the habit of burrowing, continually mixes the marsh mud, just as soil is mixed and aerated by earthworms. The fiddlers, in fact, play the same role in the marsh as earthworms do inland.

During the breeding season, the purpose of the male's fiddle is revealed. The male stands next to his burrow, waving the claw frantically, if rhythmically, at passing females. If the male manages to attract a female and she approaches, he uses the claw to shove her into the burrow entrance. Together they retreat into the burrow and mate.

The edge of the fiddle is notched and bumped ever so finely. Scientists have found that these tiny irregularities in the claw—every one of them—have a distinct purpose in courtship rituals. Since the burrow is the site of the mating, the male crabs are very territorial, and constantly contesting rights to particular burrows. They often engage in physical combat, which although it may look violent is so highly ritualized the crabs seldom hurt one another. During the combat, the

Male fiddler crabs engage in ritual combat for the right to possess a burrow, located just behind them. Ownership of a burrow means a male may be able to entice a female to mate. The combats are complicated affairs as the males bump specific ridges and knobs on their big claws against one another.

pint-size battlers bump and rub the projections and notches on their claws together, rather than use their pincers aggressively.

Like its relative the ghost crab, the fiddler spends most of its time out of the water. To breathe in such surroundings, the fiddler has gone the ghost crab one better. Not only does the fiddler have gills, but also a rudimentary lung, which if kept damp enables its owner to breathe air.

Fiddler crabs shun the cold. Where winter weather is severe, they retire into their burrows and enter a state resembling hibernation.

*The mounds of dirt outside this burrow show that a fiddler crab has been digging in the mud. Marshes and tidal flats sometimes host thousands upon thousands of these small crabs. Because they flee underground at the slightest disturbance, however, the crabs often escape notice.*

Near or even among the burrows of the fiddlers sometimes can be seen holes of a much larger diameter. These belong to the marsh crab (*Sesarma reticulatum*). The crab is brown, with yellow claws. Its shell, or carapace, is two or three inches across and has a distinctly square shape.

Several marsh crabs will share the same burrow, which usually is located near cordgrass, their main food. The marsh crabs are not exclusively vegetarian, however, because they also attack and eat the smaller fiddlers.

Because of their association with the cordgrass, the marsh crabs are found only in the low-marsh zone. They range from Cape Cod south. A similar and related crab, *Sesarma cinereum,* has colonized the upland edge of the upper marsh zone, where it can be found under driftwood and debris. Seldom venturing into the low marsh, this crab ranges from Maryland south.

## SHRIMP

South of Maine, the salt-marsh creeks—as well as mosquito-control ditches—are the home of the inch-long grass shrimp (*Palaemonetes vulgaris*). Translucent, with brown spots, the shrimp blends perfectly with the bottom and is seen mostly when it is on the move, flitting among the cordgrass, which provides its main diet.

The mangroves at the very tip of Florida are the nursery for the commercially prized pink shrimp (*Penaeus setiferus*). The young shrimp do not hatch in the mangroves but in the sea a hundred miles south, near the Dry Tortugas. After hatching, the shrimp begin an incredible migration across the water to the mangroves. Minute motes that individually scarcely are visible to the unaided eye, the shrimp travel mostly after dark, in great swarms that cloud the water. Sheltered in the mangroves, the shrimp grow until almost mature, then begin their return to the Dry Tortugas, where they themselves reproduce.

## MUSSELS

The large mussel that is prominently seen in salt marshes as far south as Georgia is the ribbed species (*Modiolus demissus*). Its brown shell, prominently ribbed, is about three inches long. The mussels grow in clumps, and attach to one another with strong threads secreted by glands in the foot. The mussel's anchor, called the byssus, sticks both under and out of water, whatever the temperature, and even when storm waves surge into the marsh.

Adaptations to marsh life are particularly graphic in the mussel. It lives throughout the low-marsh zone, in fact, anywhere in the marsh that is flooded daily by the incoming tide. The mussel feeds when under water by filtering out organic particles with a sophisticated sorting system. The particles are sifted by size in the gills. Particles which are edible and small enough to pass through the digestive system are retained. The mud, sand, and overly large particles are glued together with mucus and expelled.

With the passage of time the rejected materials build up around the mussels, which would be covered if they did not move upward. The hummocks seen in much of the low-marsh zone usually are clumps of mussels atop heaps of their waste.

Ribbed mussels have been able to survive even in the raised parts of the low marsh because they can live while exposed to air several hours daily. No other bivalve—that is, a mollusk with a hinged shell, like a clam—lives on such high ground in the marsh.

One of the reasons the mussel tolerates exposure is that it cups a bit of sea water in its shell even after the tide has retreated. It can do this because it always positions itself so that all the water will not drain from the shell. When exposed, the mussel leaves its shell slightly agape, enough for the opening to be visible. Air enters the shell, and an exchange of oxygen is made between it and the mussel's own little bit of the ocean. The mussel then taps the oxygen supply in the water, which lasts until the tide advances again.

## SNAILS

A common marsh mollusk found all along the coast has adapted to the tides in a manner exactly opposite to that of the mussel, at least as far as breathing is concerned. The common salt-marsh snail (*Melampus bidentatus*) breathes air when adult, so it must stay out of reach of the incoming tides. Because the snail lives almost entirely in the upper marsh zone, it is not vulnerable to the full impact of the tides. Even so, the marsh snail has an inner clock that warns it of approaching water. Before the tide arrives, the snail ascends high up the stalks of the salt-meadow hay, and stays there, quite dry, until the tide recedes.

The snails' internal clocks also come into play when it is time for reproduction. Marsh snails must leave their eggs where they will be swept out to sea, because the hatchling larvae are aquatic and breathe by means of gills. Alerted by their clocks, the snails stick their minuscule egg masses to the stems of salt hay, so that the next spring tide will carry them off to sea. After hatching, the larvae swim with the plankton until, in about a month, they return to a marsh, where they develop into the adult form.

Because of their need to breathe air and at the same time to leave their eggs for the tide, marsh snails inhabit a belt that is precisely bounded—on one hand by the farthest reach of the spring tide, on the other by the part of the marsh which is under water for much of the day. Within these limits, the snails flourish, so that within just a square yard, scores, even hundreds of them, can be found. During cold weather or on very hot summer days the snails may not be particularly evident, despite their abundance. To escape heat or cold they bury themselves in the mud.

Another small snail inhabits the quiet corners of the marsh, where not even wavelets disturb the water. This species is the lined or southern periwinkle (*Littorina irrorata*), a relative of the periwinkles of the rocky shore. The inch-long light brown shell of the lined periwinkle has a sharp apex, and interrupted reddish-brown lines marking its whorls.

Until not too many years ago, the lined periwinkle was purely a southern species, but increasingly it has invaded the northern half of the coast, now as far as Massachusetts. The lined periwinkle is essentially aquatic. When exposed to the air, it guards against drying by closing the opening of its shell with a "door" of tough, horny material.

The shellfish of the salt marshes have analogues in the mangroves. Roving the mangrove roots just above the water are angulate periwinkles (*Littorina angulifera*). They are the same size as their marsh relatives, and have a brownish shell that is inscribed with fine spiral lines. The shell opening is edged with white.

## OYSTERS

Clinging to the roots under the surface of the water are the small coon oysters (*Ostrea frons*). Red to purple in color, the shell of the coon oyster is not even two inches long. So thick are the growths of oysters, which sometimes are exposed during low tides, that they resemble fruit drooping from the tree roots. Early Spanish explorers, in fact, called the mangroves "oyster trees," and circulated tales about how the shellfish climbed among the branches.

# REPTILES

Marshes and mangroves host a population of reptiles that is as fascinating and spectacular as that of any inland habitat. Most of the serpents already mentioned thrive in the backwaters. But the two habitats considered here also have a number of snakes peculiar to them and unusually interesting.

The marshes of central Florida, for example, are inhabited by a rare version of the common water snake that uses the burrows of fiddler crabs. The Atlantic salt-marsh snake (*Natrix sipedon taentia*) is an extremely slender creature, usually less than two feet long, with two pair of stripes, one tan, the other yellow, on each side of the body. The rest of the back has dark blotches. The salt-marsh snake is a shy animal, unlike most water snakes, and quickly hides in the crab burrows if alarmed. Salt-marsh snakes also take up permanent residence in some burrows. So rare is the serpent that fewer than three dozen specimens are known to science, but it still may be spied by an alert marsh explorer.

A relative of the salt-marsh snake inhabits the mangrove swamps of southern Florida. The mangrove water snake (*Natrix sipedon compressicauda*) is the only water snake of extreme southern Florida that lives in salt water, and seldom anywhere else. It is much slimmer than the cottonmouth, which also can be abundant in saline surroundings, and lacks the latter's large, wide head. The mangrove snake varies greatly in color, from red to green with brown spots.

From the mangroves to Cape Cod, the backwaters are the home of a small turtle famed as a delicacy, the diamondback terrapin (*Malaclemys terrapin*). The name of this turtle comes from the markings on the upper part of its shell, which is about a half foot long. The diamond markings, plus the light spots on its slate-colored head distinguish this animal, which, although not a true sea turtle, lives almost entirely in salt or brackish water. The terrapin is not as common as it once was, because it is extremely sensitive to the pollution which has fouled so much of our coastal area.

Contrasting with the terrapin, the snapping turtle (*Chelydra serpentina*), which often inhabits the brackish waters at the rear of the marsh or the black mangrove zone, can survive in partly polluted sur-

*The diamondback terrapin, an increasingly rare salt-marsh turtle, has exquisite markings. Its feet are much more strikingly webbed than those of most North American freshwater turtles but are not paddle-like like the feet of sea turtles.*

roundings. The snapper of coastal areas is the same rough, tough species as lives in ponds, rivers, and wetlands inland. It can grow to more than a foot and a half long, not counting its tail, and a few extra-large snappers have reached over eighty pounds. Even on the average, snapping turtles are very large, and frequently weigh about twenty-five pounds. On hatching, however, the turtle has a shell that is only an inch long.

The snapping turtle has sacrificed the ability to pull its head entirely into the shell in favor of big, powerful jaws and a long neck. These help the turtle catch prey, which ranges from waterfowl to insects. The turtle also stuffs itself on vegetable matter.

Although capable of delivering a nasty bite, the snapper is not nearly the terror many people believe. It cannot, for example, bite a broomstick in half, a common old story. Nor is it always looking for a battle. A snapping turtle stepped upon while on the bottom more likely than not will try to escape. On land, not the favorite surroundings of this aquatic creature, it is much more aggressive, darting out its head and trying to catch a piece of its opponent.

The southernmost of our mangrove swamps are the home of North America's most awesome reptile, the American crocodile (*Crocodylus acutus*). The Everglades area south of Miami marks the northern limits of this animal's range which includes some of the Caribbean islands, Mexico, and part of South America. In Florida—and, indeed, in most of its range—the crocodile is very rare, but is still seen occasionally by people who boat deep in the mangroves. Although South American crocodiles sometimes are more than twenty feet long, the species is smaller in Florida, but even there reaches a length of more than a dozen feet. Gray in color, the crocodile has a markedly slender snout, distinguishing it from the American alligator (*Alligator mississipiensis*), which sometimes comes into the marshes and seaside swamps.

Ranging from North Carolina to Florida, the alligator is more characteristic of freshwater habitats, but also visits the seaside. In fact, alligators inhabit some of the southeastern sea islands, and even a few of the Florida Keys. Primarily, the alligators in the salt marshes and mangroves are there in search of food—crabs, for example—rather than a place to live. Since the alligator has become more numerous, a result of good conservation in recent years, it is much more frequently seen, near the sea as well as in its other homes.

The snout of the alligator, which has a black hide when adult, is broad and rounded at the tip, unlike that of the crocodile. People who get close enough—not advised, really, because there is considerable danger in the approach—can see another difference between the two species. The fourth tooth in the crocodile's lower jaw remains visible when the mouth is shut. Interesting to observe from a distance, these big reptiles should be left alone, for they have caused serious injury and even death.

# BIRDS

Most of the shorebirds already mentioned are seen in the marshes and to a large degree in the mangroves, although because of their south-

*Alligators sometimes live very close to the shore. While they usually spend most of the time in fresh water, they will move into brackish and salt waters to catch crabs.*

ernmost location, the latter also are inhabited by some gorgeous tropical species not present elsewhere along the coast. Among these is the roseate spoonbill (*Ajaia ajaja*), a pink bird, three feet high on its long legs, with a paddle-shaped yellow bill a half foot long.

The odd-shaped bill is an adaptation for feeding in the mangrove shallows. The bill is extremely sensitive, so that the spoonbill can feel creatures as small as minnows and water insects when it passes the organ, slightly open, through the water. At the touch of prey, the bird flips back its head and swallows its meal.

Largest wading bird in the mangroves and, in fact, in North America, is the great white heron (*Ardea occidentalis*). Four feet tall, the heron has an immense wing span, almost six feet from tip to tip. It is snow white, with yellow legs and bill. It can be distinguished from the smaller but equally white common egret by the color of the legs, which in the common species are shiny black.

Most Atlantic salt marshes have populations of rails, smaller relatives of the cranes, which resemble chickens on long legs. Rails, which generally retreat south from the northern coast in winter, have very long toes that enable them to run over vegetation matted on the water. Although rails can swim, they more commonly skitter through the marsh grass. Movement through the dense grass is permitted by their very narrow bodies. These birds, in fact, are responsible for the expression "as thin as a rail."

Largest of the rails living in salt marshes is the clapper (*Rallus longirostris*), grayish-brown with a long but rather thick bill. It is a foot long, with a wingspan of about twenty inches. The Virginia rail (*Rallus limicola*) is smaller, also grayish brown. Rails usually hunker down in the grass, and are seldom seen unless flushed by boat. Their presence is more often than not indicated by their calls—harsh, clicking, cackling noises.

Two sparrows are especially common in salt marshes. One is the sharp-tailed sparrow (*Ammospiza caudacuta*), the other the seaside sparrow (*Ammospiza maritima*). At a glance they look alike—small grayish-brown birds—and to make identification harder they often flock together. The seaside sparrow, however, has a yellow line in front of its eye, and the other species has considerable orange on its face. When flushed, both species behave the same. The bird flits through the air for a short distance, then quickly drops back into the shelter of the grass.

The marsh grasses are especially important to the sparrows in the spring, when they breed. Grass not only provides concealment but also building materials for the nest, which is placed amid tussocks or right on the ground not far above the highest tides.

Small birds such as sparrows are among the prey of the marsh hawk (*Circus cyaneus*). It is the big, dark brown bird with a conspicuous white rump seen sailing at low altitude back and forth over the marsh. With the white patch standing out against its body, this hawk with a long tail and long, rounded wings, is easy to identify. No other American hawk resembles it.

Marsh hawks summer on the northern half of the coast and winter farther south. Almost no healthy marsh is without its hawks, some of which seem ever-present as they patrol in search of something to eat. They consume a variety of animals, mostly rodents, but some birds, and even insects.

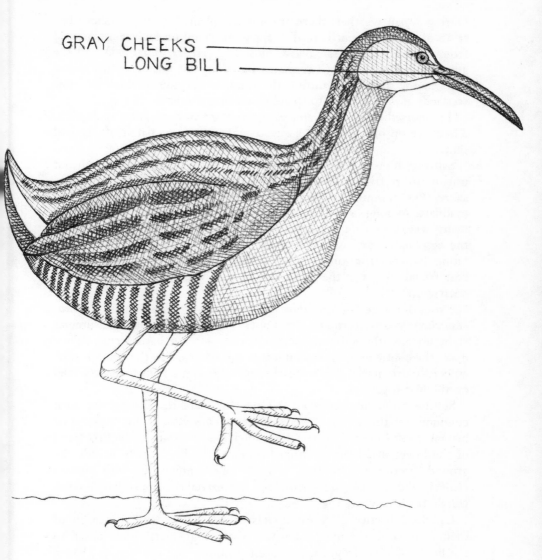

GRAY CHEEKS
LONG BILL

*Virginia rail.*

# INSECTS

During warm weather, there are insects aplenty in salt marshes. The truth of this statement is readily apparent to anyone who has suffered from the bites of the salt marsh mosquito (*Aedes sollicitans*) and the greenheaded horseflies (*Tabanus*). These are by far the worst insect pests in the marsh and during the summer become so thick in some wetlands, it is impossible to spend much time there.

The horseflies are large and sport great green eyes, their trademark. They live on blood and find a ready target on any patch of exposed skin.

Salt-marsh mosquitoes may range some distance from the marsh but usually are restricted to about a half-dozen miles inland from the seashore. The mosquitoes breed all summer long, dropping their eggs on mudflats. As long as the mud is damp, the eggs will survive, even for many weeks. Once a flat is covered by a very high tide or rainwater, the eggs hatch explosively into "wrigglers," mosquito larvae. Besides biting humans, the salt-marsh mosquito causes great harm to man's best friend, for it is the intermediate host which spreads the canine heartworm.

Ground crickets (*Nemobius*) and meadow grasshoppers (*Conocephalus*) swarm through the upper marsh zone from midsummer right up into the autumn, vanishing only after a hard freeze. They make the continual chirping hum that can be heard in the background, especially from late afternoon through the night. These insects feed on the marsh grasses.

Several kinds of beetles inhabit the salt marshes. Among the most common are the water scavenger beetle (*Enochrus*), an oval-shaped brown insect about a quarter inch long that lives at the highest parts of the lower marsh zone. Other beetles of the low marsh include the ground beetles (Carabidae) and the well-known ladybird beetles (Coccinellidae). The last-mentioned are extremely dependent on the marsh, for it is where they breed.

Ladybird beetles must eat aphids to reproduce, and in search of them rove from the upland borders of the high marsh zone down to the limits of the cordgrass. As autumn approaches, the beetles change their diet to pollen, which provides the nourishment they need to hibernate during the winter. The flowers of the late-blooming cordgrass and other marsh grasses are a prime source of pollen for the beetles.

North of Florida, the cordgrass teems with a bright green insect known as the plant bug (*Trigonotylus*). Measuring about a quarter of an inch, with spindly legs and antennae as long as its body, this insect belongs to a large group known as the "true bugs." Like the others, the plant bug folds its wings flat on its back when resting and has sucking mouthparts, with which it drains the juices from the cordgrass.

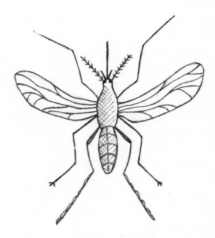

*Salt-marsh mosquito.*

# 7

## *Where to Go, What to Do*

It is no secret that the natural world of the Atlantic coast has been terribly diminished by a host of human activities, worst of all pollution of the sea and excessive development of the shore. Efforts are underway all along the coast to combat and clean up pollution, and some have been successful. In a few areas, such as the Florida mangroves, development destructive to the environment has been curbed, but most places it proceeds apace.

Even where development does not damage the environment, however, it often renders the seashore inaccessible to the vast majority of people. From Maine to the Keys, beaches have been fenced, posted or otherwise sealed off, except to people who can afford to own or rent shoreline property. Shore communities have been squeezed by seaside-property owners on one hand and hordes of inland residents seeking ocean access on the other. So municipal beaches, woefully overcrowded, have been restricted to local populaces.

Increasingly, legal challenges have been mounted by both individuals and organizations against restricted seashores. Government agencies are seeking to obtain more public waterfront. Until changes occur, however, people who want to enjoy the natural wonders of the seashore to the fullest may have to work a little to find the best access to the beach.

## WHO OWNS THE BEACH?

Several states along the Atlantic seaboard consider the intertidal region to be public. These states are: Connecticut, Florida, Maryland, New Jersey, New York, North Carolina, Rhode Island, South Carolina, and

Georgia. The remaining states permit private ownership down to the sublittoral. In the states listed above, however, no one can legally keep you off the intertidal beach—that is, as long as you can get there. The problem is not always one of private beaches, but more pointedly, the difficulty of reaching the shore.

Long stretches of allegedly public beach are effectively barred to visitors because the land behind the shore is private and lacks easements. To make matters worse, in some places legitimate easements have been illegally or deceivingly posted to keep unsuspecting outsiders away. A favorite device of tricksters who attempt this maneuver is to erect a "no trespassing" sign on their land adjacent to a road or path to the beach, implying that the thoroughfare itself is private.

Not infrequently, moreover, there are access points that have been virtually forgotten, except by a few local people. Often a thorough check of a municipality's planning or zoning documents will reveal the existence of beach easements, out of the way or long unmarked.

Many municipal beaches which have been improved by the use of federal funds are legally open to nonresidents, although this fact seldom is advertised. Very often, however, the difficulty lies in finding a place to park the car. Most municipal beaches have small parking lots, with the automobiles of residents given priority.

## STATE NATURAL AREAS

Federal and state beaches, parks, and preserves are the best bets for people seeking convenient access to sizable natural tracts on the seashore. Among those operated by states are several with truly remarkable natural features. Here is a select group suggested by state park agencies:

*Maine* offers Reid State Park, described by parks officials there as the most beautiful ocean-front park in the state. With 800 acres, the park has a mile and a half of beachfront, featuring sand beaches tucked among outcroppings of granite, a fine example of the drowned northern coastline. Conifer forest comes close to the shore along much of the beach. To reach this park, take Route 1 north 50 miles from Portland to Woolwich, then turn east on Route 127 to Georgetown. The park is open year round, although not always to vehicles when there is heavy snow.

*New Hampshire* parks authorities recommend Odiorne Point State Park in the community of Rye. It consists of 136 acres, with a mile of beach. The shore consists largely of rocks, with marvelous tide pools. Marshes lie behind the beach. The park has an interpretive center and is open year around. It is accessible from Interstate 95 and U.S. 1.

*Massachusetts* has an abundance of both rocky and sandy shores, both of which are found at Plum Island State Reservation, 72 acres at the tip of Plum Island, 40 miles north of Boston. With the open Atlantic on one side and Ipswich Bay on the other, the island has varied habitats but is especially famous for its tide pools, among the best on the coast. It is accessible from Route 1A. The roads of the park are not open to vehicles in winter.

*Rhode Island* offers a fine barrier beach in the Ninigret Conservation area, which has a typical salt pond behind the sand barrier. The area, off Scenic Route 1A, east of Westerly is noted for its spectacular surf.

*Connecticut*, the north shore of Long Island Sound, has few really wild beaches. At Hammonasset State Beach, on Route 1 in Madison, however, an effort has been made to restore dunes behind a two-mile beachfront. The park, within 900 acres, offers a small but good example of rocky coast; regenerated, artificially reconstructed dunes; and extensive salt marshes. It is an excellent site for observing autumn hawk migrations. The exit for the beach is marked on the nearby Connecticut Turnpike.

*New York* has natural seaside areas even close to New York City, including Jones Beach State Park, just 33 miles from the metropolis. The park has six miles of ocean beach, backed by bird sanctuaries, where in season terns and gulls nest in large numbers. Winter brings considerable numbers of scaup and other waterfowl. The beach is reached from New York City via three parkways, the Meadowbrook, Wantagh, and Robert Moses.

*New Jersey*, with a heavily developed coastline, nevertheless has an excellent example of barrier beach at Island Beach State Park, south of Seaside Heights. Ten miles long, the park has two natural areas, separated by a recreational section. Behind the park is Barnegat Bay, rich in water birds. In front is the open ocean. Thus the park extends from the water's edge through the beach, primary dunes, and interdune zone, to a bay with marshes. Its nature center is open in summer. Migratory bird life is plentiful during the right seasons. The park is reached from Exit 82 on the Garden State Parkway, via Route 37 east to Seaside Heights. From there, the road leads south to the park gate.

*Delaware* park officials recommend Cape Henlopen State Park, which is on a point jutting into the mouth of Delaware Bay, east of Lewes. The park has waterfront on both the bay and the open ocean. Mudflats and sandbars are prominent on the bay side, where in season, extensive colonies of terns and other sea birds can be seen. The park is also noted for its "walking dunes," a vivid example of how the sands of the beach continually shift and move. The "great dune," 80 feet high, is one of the tallest on the entire coast. The park is accessible off Route 1, or can be reached from New Jersey via the Cape May–Lewes ferry.

*Maryland,* in its Calvert Cliffs State Park, has one of the nation's finest sites for the discovery of fossil marine animals. The park, which also has extensive inland tracts in its 1,177 acres, includes part of a 30-mile stretch of cliffs overlooking the ocean. The cliffs, an upraised portion of what 15 million years ago was sea bed, contain a treasure trove of fossils. Six hundred different species have been identified. The most noted are prehistoric sharks, which left their teeth in abundance. No digging for fossils is allowed on the cliffs, which are eroding, but many wash up on the beach. Visitors who find them can take them home. The park fronts on lower Chesapeake Bay, just north of the mouth of the Patuxent River, and 14 miles south of Prince Frederick, on Routes 2 and 4.

*Virginia* operates Seashore State Park at the mouth of the Chesapeake Bay, off Route 60, at Cape Henry. The park is located on an important route for migratory waterfowl, and not very far from the Dismal Swamp National Wildlife Refuge, which lies inland. The park offers an excellent chance to observe the meeting of the great Chesapeake estuary with the open waters of the Atlantic.

*South Carolina* boasts Huntington Beach State Park, near the community of Litchfield Beach. The park, just off Route 17, contains 2,500 acres, mostly undeveloped, with plants and animals characteristic of the southeastern coastal plain. The fauna includes 85 alligators, which often are easy to see, in a freshwater lagoon near the entrance to the facility. The park's ocean beach, backed by a good example of maritime scrub, has spring nesting colonies of terns and shore birds.

*Georgia* operates Sapelo, one of the large sea islands, and the site of several scientific institutions, along with a vast complex of salt marshes. Access to the island is by boat, weekends, restricted to a small number of people on a first-come, first-served basis. The boat can be boarded at the community of Meridian, reached by traveling east on Route 99 off Interstate 95. On reaching the island, boat passengers are taken on a tour over boardwalks built above the marshes. Information can be obtained from the Georgia Department of Natural Resources in Atlanta.

*Florida* is the site of the first underwater state park in the United States, on Key Largo. The John Pennekamp Coral Reef State Park, together with the neighboring Key Largo Coral Reef Marine Sanctuary, provides a fine example of the coral coast, with mangroves behind the beaches. The area takes in more than 170 square nautical miles of mangroves, coral reefs, and beds of sea grass, backed by limestone uplands.

# NATIONAL SEASHORES AND OTHER FEDERAL AREAS

Some of the finest natural areas on the coast are administered by the federal government. These include a small number of national seashores and parks, and a string of national wildlife refuges. The refuges are operated by the United States Fish and Wildlife Service, the parks and seashores by the National Park Service. Both agencies belong to the United States Department of the Interior.

The wildlife refuges serve primarily as breeding, resting, feeding, and wintering grounds for migratory waterfowl but also support large numbers of other animals. More than three dozen exist along the coast, so only a portion of these—some typical examples—will be described here. All parks and seashores will be mentioned.

*Acadia National Park*, on Mount Desert Island and adjoining areas in Maine, is not very large as National Parks go, only about 41,000 acres, but spectacular. It has jagged cliffs, battered by surf —a true glacial landscape. Within the park, on Mount Desert Island, is Cadillac Mountain, at 1,530 feet the highest point on the Atlantic shoreline. The park contains true wilderness, and deep forests that advance down to the edge of the sea. It is reached from Bar Harbor, site of the park headquarters.

*Cape Cod National Seashore* stretches from Chatham, at the elbow of the Cape, to Provincetown, at the tip, 30 miles of dune-backed, surf-swept beach. Behind the dunes are marshes, pines, and freshwater ponds. The National Seashore takes in virtually all of the Cape's Great Beach, dominated by the towering bluffs of a long glacial moraine. Headquarters are located at South Wellfleet.

*Fire Island National Seashore*, on the south shore of Long Island, is less than an hour's drive east of New York City. Located on a narrow barrier island, the area remains wild, despite its urban location. It has large dunes, marshes, and a magnificent sandy beach. Seashore headquarters are at Patchogue.

*Brigantine National Wildlife Refuge*, a vast tract of marshes less than a dozen miles from Atlantic City, New Jersey, supports hundreds of thousands of waterfowl on its almost 20,000 acres during the migratory seasons. The refuge is known for its brant, small geese somewhat similar in coloration to the Canada goose, but quite rare. The refuge is one of the best salt-marsh areas on the northern half of the coast.

*Assateague Island National Seashore* begins just south of Ocean City, Maryland, across a channel broken through the thin barrier island by a storm not many years ago. The seashore shares the island, part in Maryland, part in Virginia, with a state park and a national wildlife refuge. Here is a beautifully preserved barrier beach, with the full variety of sandy beach and dune plants and animals, and some pluses. Introduced on the island in colonial times, and running wild since then, are ponies; an Asian deer, the sika, has inhabited the island since a herd was released there by Boy Scouts in the 1920s. The island has the full spectrum of sandy-beach zones, from the ocean to back bay and salt marsh. During the autumn and winter, Assateague is one of the best sites on the coast to watch migratory waterfowl. Seashore headquarters are at Snow Hill, Maryland.

*Chincoteague National Wildlife Refuge* is sandwiched between two portions of the National Seashore. Behind the beach is a maze of marshes and pools, where waterfowl concentrate. Winter brings migratory Canada and snow geese, plus whistling swans, scaup, canvasbacks, and mergansers. The winter population leaves by April, and shortly afterward resident waterfowl—black ducks, mallards, gadwall, and teal—begin to breed. The headquarters of the refuge, which has an excellent visitor center, is at the community of Chincoteague, Virginia.

*Cape Hatteras National Seashore* begins just south of famed Nag's Head, and runs south all along the Outer Banks of North Carolina, preserving this remarkable stretch of coastline. Headquarters are at Manteo, North Carolina.

*Cape Lookout National Seashore,* separated by a narrow channel from Hatteras, continues the federal protection of the Outer Banks. Together, the two national seashores cover more than 100 miles of these marvelous barrier islands. Cape Lookout, unlike Hatteras, is not accessible by car, only by boat. Ferry service is available for foot passengers. The headquarters for this new seashore is at Beaufort, North Carolina.

*Blackbeard Island National Wildlife Refuge* is one of several located on Georgia's sea islands. The refuge takes up 6,000 acres, including nine miles of sandy beach, a virgin forest of pine, and fresh water wetlands. The island is separated from the mainland by 18 miles of marsh and water, so is reachable only by boat. Arrangements can be made through the United States Fish and Wildlife Service Refuge Manager in Savannah.

*Cumberland Island National Seashore,* with headquarters at St. Marys, Georgia, is reached by ferry. This large sea island has a dozen miles of beach, salt marsh, freshwater sloughs, dunes, and forests of live oaks, palmettos, and pines. There are wading birds and waterfowl, turtles, and a number of alligators, which inhabit the sloughs behind the beach. The beach, 1,000 feet wide in some places, is full of shells, especially large whelks. Offshore, pelicans are common during the warmer months.

*Canaveral National Seashore* is a strip of barrier beach north of the John F. Kennedy Space Center in Florida. It teems with wading birds; thousands of ducks arrive in the winter; and shore birds abound. The seashore, with headquarters in Titusville, shares some of its 57,628 acres with the adjacent Merritt Island National Wildlife Refuge.

*Merritt Island National Wildlife Refuge,* like the seashore, is a wild natural area in the shadow of the Kennedy space complex. The proximity of the space center, however, has not discouraged wildlife. Alligators, for instance, thrive on the refuge, and it is possible that the rare Florida race of the cougar may still be found there. The refuge, behind the barrier beach, is one of the northernmost outposts of large mangrove swamps. The headquarters also is in Titusville.

*Biscayne National Monument* takes in a group of Florida's keys north of Key Largo. Biscayne Bay is to the west, and the open ocean on the eastern side of the monument, which offers a good variety of coral coast habitats. The headquarters is inland, in Homestead.

*Everglades National Park* also has a Homestead headquarters. This park, covering more than 1,400,000 acres, is the largest remaining subtropical wilderness area in the United States. The "glades" themselves are in the interior, and are flooded prairies, cut by sloughs, dotted with hummocks and cypress swamps. The coastal portion of the park contains an immense area of mangroves, by far the largest in the country.

Additional information on places to see nature at the seashore can be obtained from the National Park Service or Fish and Wildlife Service in Washington, or state conservation agencies. Most states also have Audubon societies or similar organizations that will help. An excellent source for information on marine environments or affairs anywhere along the Atlantic coast is the American Littoral Society, a nonprofit conservation organization located on Sandy Hook, in Highlands, New Jersey. The society has chapters in several states.

## SEASHORE CRAFTS

The seashore is a collector's paradise. All sorts of items, natural and made by man, are cast up upon the shore. Driftwood and shells, of course, are favorites. It is fine to take both, and causes no harm to the environment, as long as the shells are not still part of living animals. Many types of mollusks have become rare because shell fanciers have overcollected them while the animals were still living. The same is true of coral. Living coral should never be taken. Even dead coral should not be removed from a reef, because although it is no longer alive it remains as an important part of the reef's foundation. It is perfectly fine, on the other hand, to take home pieces of coral found on the beach.

Casual shell collecting can be great fun. Serious shell collecting requires considerable dedication but can be a lifelong hobby that provides deep satisfaction. It even can be profitable, because fortunes have been paid for rare shells. There are many books, technical and popular, on how to collect, prepare, and display shells.

Shells also can be made into many decorative items. Some people just fill small clear bottles or brandy snifters with very small shells, and stand them on a shelf. A very attractive display piece can be made by covering a bottle with shells of various sizes and colors. When finished, it looks elaborate, but the way to do it is easy. First glue a coat of cotton to the bottle, making sure all the glass is covered. Then glue the shells, one at a time, to the cotton, fitting them so that none of the cotton remains exposed. There is no more to it.

A wall hanging can be made from a small plaque of plaster of paris, on which sand has been sprinkled and in which shells have been embedded while the mixture is wet. Shells also can be strung on mobiles.

Seaweed seems an unlikely thing to collect but can be turned into prints worthy of framing. To make one, find a portion of seaweed that is undamaged and in good color. Place it in a bowl of water—sea water preferably, because fresh water may ruin the color of the plant.

When the seaweed is spread out in the water, remove it by slipping a sheet of white paper beneath it, and lifting it up. Be careful not to disturb the seaweed on the paper. Put the paper holding the seaweed on a thick layer of newspapers. Cover the seaweed with a clean cloth, and then with another layer of newspapers. Over these place a board, and weight the stack down with a brick, electric iron, books, or something similar. The weight will press the seaweed as it dries. If it seems to retain dampness, change newspapers and cloth. Once dry, the seaweed should stick to the paper. If not, help it out with glue. The dried seaweed then can be mounted and framed.

It is possible to make casts of the tracks that birds and other animals leave in the dry beach sand. Simply fill and cover the track with a rather thin mixture of plaster of paris, or water putty. Once the mixture dries, dig around the edges of the cast and lift it out. The negative of the track will be preserved on the plaster or putty.

## NATURAL JOURNAL

Over the years, even the months, you can accumulate a surprising amount of interesting natural history information by keeping a journal of trips to the seashore. The key to a good nature journal is writing down the observations as you see them, not later. Afterward, the account can be fleshed out.

A journal is best kept in a looseleaf binder six by nine inches or thereabouts in size. It is a good idea to cover the notebook with oilcloth or some other waterproof material. Use lined paper and a pen with a fine point and waterproof ink.

A new page should be used to begin notes for each trip. At the top of the page, write down the year. On the first line note the date and place. Below, jot down the type of weather, with air temperature and, if possible, water temperature. Both can be taken with a regular outdoor thermometer.

Make sure you have taken along a watch so that when an observation is noted, the time can be jotted down in the margin next to it. Be as precise as possible, especially about the number of things seen, and where the subjects were when the notes were taken.

At the end of each trip, a summary section—entitled "diary," if you will—should be placed at the end of the account. This is the place to briefly describe the overall trip, background conditions, and your reactions. You might note, for instance, that "This is the first time I have seen mallards on the east marsh."

In the diary, you can make comparisons with data taken in the past. It is very interesting, for example, to see if the same species turn up under similar conditions at a particular season, year after year. You may find that migrating birds such as ospreys and herons will show up precisely at the same location on the same dates each autumn for several years in a row.

# CRABBING

Fresh blue crabs are one of the tastiest edibles that you can find at the edge of the sea, where creatures fit for the dinner platter abound. Crabs are not hard to catch, at least for people who are patient. There are two tried-and-true methods.

One is with a dip net and bait line. Any net with a small mesh and long handle will work. The best bait is a chicken neck, which is firm enough not to crumble in the water and for the crab to hold on to. Tie the bait with a strong cord and lower it into the water. When a crab nibbles on it, you will feel a series of sharp tugs. Slowly raise the bait. The crab will probably follow it to the surface, and even hold tight. When the crab is within reach, slide the net under it and scoop it up. Move slowly until ready for the scoop, then do it as fast as you can.

Another way to catch crabs is with a collapsible trap, lowered to the bottom on a cord. There are several kinds of strong wire mesh, shaped like a box or star. The bait is tied to the center of the trap. When the trap is lowered to the bottom, it unfolds. By pulling up quickly, you can close the trap. Wait until a crab busies itself with the bait, and haul it in. Sometime several crabs can be caught at one time in this way.

The old Maryland method for steaming crabs is the finest way to cook them. You need a steamer—a large pot with a false bottom, perforated and about two inches from the real bottom. Fill the space between the two bottoms with a cup of vinegar and a cup of water. Bring it to a boil. Place the crabs in layers on the false bottom. Make sure the crabs are alive, guaranteeing freshness when steamed. Sprinkle each layer with a touch of salt and seafood seasoning—special seasoning for crabs is available in some food stores. Let the crabs steam for a half hour. Then remove them and eat them hot. You may want to use a hammer—the traditional implement is a wooden mallet—to crack the claws of the crab. A word of caution should be heeded. Never allow steamed crabs to come in contact with any item—such as a basket—that has held uncooked crabs. Bacteria from the uncooked crabs can contaminate the cooked batch.

## COQUINA DELIGHT

The tiny coquina clams that live at the edge of the surf make the best of all clam broth. Simply put a cup or two of these little shellfish in a pot—after washing them free of sand, of course—cover with water, and turn on the heat. Once the water boils, turn the heat down to a simmer. After 10 minutes, take the broth off the heat, strain out the clams, and enjoy it.

## CLAM RAKING

The easiest way to obtain larger clams is to use a clam rake. This is a long-handled tool with long, narrow tines, very sharp. Raking should be done in water that is at least waist deep, to avoid having to cope with old, empty shells, which are washed up to the shallows. Rake just a few inches below the surface of the bottom, until you feel the tines hit the hard shell of a clam. Then all you have to do is bend over, feel around the rake with your hand until you touch the clam, and pick it up. Clams can be eaten raw, with cocktail sauce, vinegar, or lemon; fried; or made into chowder. An exceptionally tasty way to cook clams is to wash them, then place them on a grill above a charcoal fire. Let them cook for a minute or so, until the shells open. Then eat them on the half shell with the same type of topping used on raw clams. Cooked this way, clams retain the delicate flavor they have when eaten raw but are hot and, for many people, more palatable than when gulped down alive.

## CHECK THE LAW FIRST

Before taking any sort of marine animal—for collecting or cooking—check local laws regarding limits, seasons, the need for licenses, and health hazards. This way you protect yourself and cooperate with conservation, helping protect the natural resource of the sea's bounty.

# INDEX